#DIARY
Of A Girl

A Journey From Brokenness to Wholeness

#DIARY

Of A Girl

A Journey From Brokenness to Wholeness

**ANTIOCH CHRISTIAN
PUBLISHING COMPANY LTD**

Diary of a Girl

ISBN: 978-0-9893357-2-0

Editor: Paula Richards, Eagle's Eye Editing Services
"We Perfect Your Writing!"
Email: eagleseyeservices@gmail.com

Cover Design: Lydia Nicole Graphic Design
"A Simple Love For Design"
Warrens St. Michael, Barbados
Email: lydia@iamlydianicole.com
Web: www.iamlydianicole.com
Facebook: Lydia Nicole Graphic Design

Cover Photo: Amaris Harper, DLightful Media
Published by Antioch Christian Publishing Company
www.antiochpublishingcompany.com
(USA) 301-836-5053. Caribbean: 868-755-0064

Dedication

I want to dedicate this book to all of my single sisters. Know that you may be fighting a battle, but you are not fighting alone. You may be wondering; should I give up? Is there still hope? Has God forgotten about me? When will I stop kissing frogs? Where is my king? I SEE YOU, BABY GIRL!!!

I believe that transparency and realness is effective in the changing of lives. The things that I have fought through were for the benefit of the kingdom, and the winning of souls for God. Dear Queen, you may have tripped along the way and your tiara may have fallen, rest assured that it's not the end. To my beautiful Queen, woman of worth, woman of value, woman of purpose, woman of God, it's just the beginning. Be encouraged.

Acknowledgements

If there's anyone more deserving of a thank you it is you Daddy God. Thank you for bringing me this far; for never giving up on me, not even the times when I was guilty of letting go of Your hands. I love you with everything I have and will continue to serve you faithfully.

Thank you Jewel Hoyte for being there every step of the way. You were there from the beginning of this project. When I first shared the idea, your faith in me, despite me not believing in myself-at the time brought great encouragement. Several nights I messaged you, probably annoying you, yet you readily helped wherever possible.

To my father, Robert Howell, your daughter is very appreciative of your support and love. You may have been absent during my childhood, but you've certainly been there since and continue to be. Thank you for always backing me 100 percent in my pursuit of purpose.

To my grandmother, Mavis Brathwaite, a heartfelt thanks for taking up the task of parenting me. Noted, it was not always easy, but you did it and I am forever grateful.

My sincere gratitude goes out to my church family. Thank you for getting onboard and being supportive spiritually and financially. I am truly appreciative.

Maria Carter, I can't thank you enough for being a part of my journey. Your continuous encouragement, your willingness to assist, I double thank you for all your help.

Paula Richards, I am endlessly honored to have you present in my life. Despite us meeting at the late stage in this process, you have impacted my life and this book tremendously. I want to thank you for that eagle eye vision (lol) and for the wisdom you have imparted.

I wish to thank all my family and friends who pitched in, whether spiritually, financially, physically, advice or even a word of- encouragement; I love you guys and appreciate all you have done.

Lastly, what would I do without you? Words cannot describe how thankful I am to my sisters-in-Christ who purchased my book. Thank you for spending your money wisely (haha) and for giving a sister t h e opportunity to make that difference in your life.

Foreword

I was deeply humbled to be asked to give a review of Diary of a Girl. From the very start of this book one could see that Shaniqua has laid herself bare for all to see, her emotions, everything, holding nothing back, something that many people are not comfortable doing. I commend her. It is my belief that this well written "Diary" of her life's trials, testings and eventual surrender to God will help many a person to discover true forgiveness and freedom as she did. There is something in this book that everyone can relate to and learn from.

Her honesty and openness serve as encouragement to other Christians who have, or are facing challenges in their own lives, not to go through alone. Shaniqua has carefully woven timely and relevant scripture to deal with each issue that came up in her life. This book is a 'must read' for all, in particular parents who will see firsthand the importance of/their love, affirmation and acceptance in the lives of their children.

Shaniqua offers valuable insight and counsel to other young ladies and singles regarding the pitfalls and platforms in relationships. You will laugh at her sometimes quirkiness and cry with her during her moments of sadness and despair.

Congratulations, Shaniqua! It is always heartening when the local Church community can read books by 'one of our own'. The Pure Sex Centre, highly recommends this book to all!! Maria M Carter dip.Th.

Once upon a time in a castle far away, there was a princess who was locked up in a dark dungeon on the bay. She was trapped what could she do? There was no escape, was there even hope? She didn't have a clue.

Night after night she was tormented by the dragon that roamed the hallways and guarded the gate; she couldn't escape; was this fate? Chains bound her physically and mentally to this castle; If she ran away, exactly where would she settle?

The windows were shut extremely tight, She was never able to see the marvelous light. She had put her trust and hope that one day A man would save her, Little did she know that she would have an encounter with the REDEEMER?

This princess expected a man of earthly stature but was surprised that salvation came from Jesus Christ the only one who mattered. The fight was on, the battle was fierce, this man called Jesus came and put the dragon in his place. The princess was rescued and the dragon defeated. No longer a slave, she was no more mistreated.

She was cleaned up, dusted off and set upon high places, Ready to serve the One, and give Him all the praises. She had been through the darkest nights But it was not in

vain, For God birthed purpose out of her pain.
She was no longer the sad broken down princess,
a mighty woman of God, a Queen on a mission.
-Shaniqua L. Howell

Contents

Introduction

Is the thought of marriage taking precedence over your relationship with Christ? Are you begging God repeatedly to send you that husband? Does it seem as if the rejection of the past keeps rearing its ugly head? Are you crying at night wondering why all of your friends are married and you are still single? Then this book is for you.

#Diary Of A Girl is my first publication and I hope that my story will be a help and a source of hope to the single female out there. This book and name were inspired after my last encounter with a guy who I allowed to break my heart. My mission was to share my thoughts and feelings to the world; to be an encouragement to all my single sisters; assuring them that they are not fighting alone. The Diary of this girl is no longer sealed but opened to the person who should decide to take a peep in.

How did I get here yet again? I thought that part of my life was over; so why does it seem like déjà vu. Why am I back here struggling with these spirits when I thought they were dealt with? How was it possible that I felt I had it all together when actually I did not? Often times as Christians, we believe within our hearts that we are completely over an issue, but somehow when we least expect it, it pops back up like a zit about to burst.

This is not your average Christian read. My goal is not to sugar coat anything I'm about to say, but to openly strip myself naked before you. This is my story, my struggles, my joy, my hurts, my pain, my blessings, my love, my heartaches and my determination. THIS IS ME. You may know my name or my address but you surely don't know my story. This is the story of the lost girl who became the woman that was eventually found; the broken down princess, who became a queen. THIS IS MY DIARY.

Chapter 1

In the Beginning

Jeremiah 1:5 *Before I formed you in the womb I knew you; before you were born I sanctified you; I ordained you a prophet to the nations.*

Even before conception, God knew me. Out of the nearly 500 million sperm that were released, He plucked me out specifically, and knew me even before I knew myself. I was chosen in Him before the foundation of the earth, despite being the result of an unplanned pregnancy, I was never a mistake.

Psalm 139:13 *For You formed my inward parts; You covered me in my mother's womb.*

Unlike what many would like to believe, I was not born a Christian. Hard to fathom, right? NO. That statement was for the believers who are under the assumption that they came out their mother's womb singing hymns and beating cymbals. As for me though, I did not. I was about to enter into a sinful and evil world, and the devil was on a mission to abort the plans God had for my life. I was born to parents who were not married, but who each had a baby girl around the age of two. They probably had no intention of being together long, furthermore, having to deal with an unplanned pregnancy. It was not their ideal choice to have me, but God was in control, and so I was born. For reasons I never understood, my mother gave me to my grandmother when I was about three months, and this is where I believe my issues started to form.

Remember I told you I was born into a sinful and evil world? Well, Satan was beginning to mold and shape me into the person he wanted me to be, so I wouldn't be able to fulfill my destiny and God given purpose on earth. I was basically raised by my grandparents. I lived with my maternal grandmother, who also had the help of her boyfriend. He was like a grandfather to me and I would also frequent my father's parents' home on the weekends. Thus, growing up as a child, in my mind, I was rejected by both my parents. How could someone give their offspring to another person? I couldn't quite understand and would constantly wonder.

You see, what made it worse was the fact that my parents were both living in the same country. In my opinion, that made matters worse on the rejection front. They both had their reasons for what they did, but as a child back then, it was hard for me to understand and so I felt as if I was unwanted. The devil does not start to work his plans when you are old as some of you may think. He zealously wants to get into our minds and filter his pollution from the time we are mere babes.

His aim is to steal, kill and destroy. This is why it is important for us to bring up our children in a godly home and teach them the ways of the Lord. The exact time can't be recalled, but I do remember at a much younger age my father deciding to leave Barbados to live abroad. Oh, how the enemy used this as another way to solidify that spirit of rejection. In my mind, the enemy was sowing seeds that would continue to grow as the years went by.

In reality, my father was leaving the island because he had to; in my mind he was leaving because he did not care, and so I felt rejected. Bear in mind that when this spirit of rejection comes, it does not enter alone, but comes bearing satanic gifts of low self-esteem, low self-worth, insecurity issues and the list goes on. Might I add that I had them all and more! Tough for a child, right? As time flew and I came into my teenage years, I grew colder, meaner, sadder, unhappier, and the stronghold rejection had on me just kept graduating to newer levels.

I hardly ever saw my Dad, probably about once every couple of years, and I still did not have a relationship with my mother. To everyone at school I was the tough girl. I was the person, who didn't have a care for anything or anyone, and was quick to fight and slow to speak. No, I was not a Christian then, so don't judge me... (lol) I was talking to my friend one day and we were reminiscing on our time spent at school. She said, "Shaniqua, you were so mean and cold." We both recounted on the things that I had done and I couldn't help but say, "God, thank you for your grace and mercy."

Many times I would sit and reflect on that lost and broken little girl who tried to mask herself. Hurt people tend to hurt people. Yes, she was absolutely right. I was, as people would say a mean girl, but I thank God for showing me the light. My grandmother did the best she could in raising me, and for that, I am extremely thankful.

My home was not one of hugs, kisses and 'I love you', but despite not hearing those words, which every child longs to hear, I still knew without a shadow of a doubt that I was loved and cared for in the only way she knew how to. It's safe to say my family was not the touchy feely type. It is somewhat difficult for someone to express love when they themselves are clueless on how to show it. Morals and values were drilled into me from a young age.

Sometimes I swore I came out of a Christian home, even though I didn't. When other girls were sneaking around and having sex, I was home 25/8 reading and watching TV. Sex was never a concern of mine. I would like a few guys, but that was it, because I would always hear my grandmother in my ears constantly saying: "Girl, sex ain't going nah where, it ain't gonna go out of style, so you cool yourself!"

My virginity was something I held dear, and I wanted to keep it that way. From the way I acted, everyone thought I was sexually active, but that was far from the truth. Allowing guys to get close to me was a big no-no; I was not about to let anyone get close enough to then leave me. To my school mates, I knew it all, I did it all, and I was the 'IT' girl. Brave, confident, bold and hard hearted. But in reality, I was masked out; for behind the entire pretense, I was shy, insecure, lost, depressed and suffered tremendously.

I was just a messed up and broken individual. Satan and his demons were chanting and shouting, *"We have this one secured!"* On the other hand, God was watching me and whispering, *"Don't you worry, my daughter, I got you, and your story will be used for My glory."* Guess who won? You guessed right.

At the age of 15, I went to Canada to spend the summer vacation with my Dad. One summer turned into four years. I loved my father without a doubt, but being away from home was killing me. Let me break it down for you. I was a people pleaser, but not in the way you may think. More than likely I surmise that it stemmed from the rejection, so I would always have a need to feel accepted and would try to please people.

I liked the idea of seeing people happy even if it meant sacrificing my needs. So after my summer vacation was over, my father asked me to stay in Canada with him. "This is the chance for me to get to know him better," I pondered. On the other hand, I was about to leave behind everything I had known for the past 15 years.

New beginnings are extremely scary, especially for a teenager. Nevertheless, in the end, I decided to stay, because like I said, I had a hard time saying no and I wanted to get to know my Dad as well. I often wondered if I could split myself in two and be in more than one place at the same time. I really wanted to stay in Canada but I also wanted to be back home with my friends and family. Impossible I know, not even Satan has that power. Only my Daddy God is omnipresent.

During my stay, there were bittersweet moments. I was getting the chance to bond with my father and my new family, but on the other hand, I was still missing home. I refused to speak to my Dad about it because I knew he loved the idea of finally getting to be with me and it would probably crush him. He was very aware and never denied that he had missed a big chunk of my childhood, and he tried his best to make up for the time he had missed.

I was privately depressed - emotionally, mentally and spiritually, without anyone knowing. My mask was becoming thicker, smiling with the world on the outside, but in turmoil inside. I was battling some demons as people may say. And then, out of nowhere, I started to self-harm. Where did it come from? I hadn't a clue at that time. It was only after becoming a Christian that God revealed to me that it was a mere spirit from the enemy assigned to take my life. For those of you who may not know what self- harming is, let me clarify.

Self-harm (also known as self-injury or self-mutilation) Is the act of deliberately causing harm to oneself either by causing a physical injury, by putting oneself in dangerous situations and/or self-neglect. Some forms that self-harm can take include: cutting, burning, biting and substance abuse.
– Greenshaw Self-harm protocol

The world sees this as a disease but the root is demonic. For people suffering from the spirit of self-harm, this may sound strange; I honestly believe they want to inflict pain to themselves, but they really don't want to die. For me, I was trying to run from what I was feeling inside, the monsters were starting to become many and I didn't know how to deal with them.

Even though I was receiving the attention I always wanted from my father, the feeling of rejection still kept its hold on me. Quite firmly I might add! The emotional and mental pain I felt was crashing down on me; I just wanted an escape. If only it was for a minute or so, the physical pain seemed like a temporary way out. Just like a junkie, I wanted a temporary fix. Not realizing that a temporary fix was just that, a temporary fix and nothing more.

When I felt drained and depressed, I took a razor or any sharp object I could find and would repeatedly cut myself until I bled and felt better. However, in spite of my wrongdoing, I was still very smart; I would cut myself in places not visible to my Dad. When I did cut visible areas, I would strategically do it within an already old scar. I was emotionally weak, and I hadn't a clue about a Jesus who would give me strength. Satan had his claws carved into my skin and was looking for ways to take me out.

In all that crazy mess, God had His hand on my life. He looked at me and could see that a message was seeping out from my mess. Just like that, the same way I started self-harming,

I finished. One day, I just decided that I had to stop and I never did it again. In my mind, I believe that in the spiritual world it all happened like this.

My Angel: Turn to God Shaniqua, you can find peace in Him.

Satan: She is important; she needs to be taken out.

God: Keep fighting, Princess.

I guess I'm a bit dramatic right? Oh well! It's my story not yours, so shut up and continue to read. (Lol)

We all deal with pain differently for we are not the same. Self-harming is more common than many of you may think and it's very important for us to ask God for the discernment that we can fight against this spirit. Many young people are struggling with self-harm and we haven't a clue. Christ said that He came to seek and save the lost, and as His followers, we should have a burning desire and passion to help the lost and helpless. Many people are hurting and fighting battles we do not know about. Helping people find a way out of the darkness should be a concern of ours. We have a duty as Christians to give hope to the hopeless, and that my friend, is pointing them to Christ, the One who gives that hope.

For those of you who are reading this and may be self-harming or on the verge of it, I implore you to STOP. God can lift any burden and give you a peace that surpasses understanding. No matter what you are going through in this season, it isn't too difficult for the Lord to handle. Right now it may seem like all is lost and there is no hope; you feel like no one understands what you're going through, and actually you are right. No man on earth can look into your eyes and say "I understand", for we may have similar struggles, but they are not the same.

Hebrews 4:15-16 For we do not have a High Priest who cannot sympathize with our weaknesses, but was in all points tempted as we are, yet without sin. Let us therefore come boldly to the throne of grace, that we may obtain mercy and find grace to help in time of need.

I can however assure you, that My Daddy, the King of kings and Lord of lords knows and understands just what you are going through. He is the hope I present to you; the One who knows every single hair on your head? He will wipe away your tears and give you strength and peace that you can never get elsewhere. He is concerned about everything that goes on in your life. Give Him a chance, for I know you will never regret it.

Psalm 147:3 He heals the brokenhearted and binds up their wounds.

Matthew 11:28-30 Come to Me, all you who labor and are heavy laden, and I will give you rest. Take My yoke upon you and learn from Me, for I am gentle and lowly in heart, and you will find rest for your souls. For My yoke is easy and My burden is light.

After going back home to Barbados for a visit, I stayed and never returned to Canada. Of course my Dad was fuming, but he got over it after a while. After all is said and done I am his princess, right? I guess by now you think that with me being home at last, I would be happy. WRONG.

I would never truly be happy until I decided to deal with the demons that tormented me at night, but I didn't know how to as yet. I was free from self-harming and back in my home country, but I was not free from the strongholds that were trying to ruin my life. My angel was battling on my behalf, but Satan was not about to give up. I was basically a threat to the kingdom of darkness. He had to take me out or keep me under his control, but thanks to God for always keeping me protected.

Now that I was home, what next was there to do? I was introduced to partying by my family and friends, and so I began to frequent the hot spots. During the day I was the insecure little girl, but at night I was the confident young woman, who seemed to have it all together. Little did they know! I did not have an identity and so I was lost. I was looking for somewhere to fit in and couldn't seem to find a place.

The demons would fight me so much that I would literally wake up on mornings with scratches on my skin. I felt hopeless and uncertain of my future and despite being in the crowd, I felt alone. Sometimes I just wanted someone to come up to me and be able to see through the entire pretense and say, "You're not ok." To be hugged and held protectively without being asked, "What's wrong?" Not saying anything, but to squeeze me tightly and hug me quietly. That lost little girl was searching for love. She was now growing into adulthood and the need for love continued to grow stronger and she wouldn't be able to handle it.

Dear Diary,

When I look back and remember that broken girl, tears begin to roll down my face. She may not have had the worst childhood, but the one thing she wanted and craved the most she couldn't find anywhere. That sad little girl was about to become a sadder adult and she didn't even know. She was hunted by demons that bombarded her soul. The outside was like a garden of roses, but the inside was a deserted pasture. EMPTY.

Chapter 2

Relationship Suicide

High School Sweetheart

His name is Ray but let's call him the high school sweetheart. We had a thing for each other in school, but it didn't work out for various reasons, one of them being my time in Canada, but now, I was home again. Somehow we got in touch and, yeah you know where I'm going with this; we ended up in a relationship. Can we say catastrophe? Was it even possible to be in a relationship the way I felt? I was plagued with rejection and low self-esteem. I had a degree in all these categories, and I was on my way to having a Bachelors.

I was an unstable individual going into a union with someone, and expecting it to work. By the way, I was still a virgin; my grandmother's words still rang throughout my head. My virginity was a treasure I possessed for a long time; it was the only thing I had control over. As this was my first actual relationship, I felt scared and helpless.

How was I supposed to love someone when I didn't even love myself? How was I supposed to love another, when I had no idea what love even was to begin with? I was starting to feel things I had never felt before. "What if I got too attached to him and then he decides to leave?" I would repeatedly contemplate.

"RUNNNNN!" was all I heard in my head, and so I did. It's very easy to run away from situations instead of dealing with them.

I was petrified of being rejected or left alone if I got too close, and so I figured I should do it first. How messed up is that, right? I never said a word to him, but ignored his calls and his visits, just running scared. Eventually he got tired and gave up. I had this conjured up theory in my mind that if he really loved me he would have fought harder. Even more messed up thinking, isn't it? I was the coward who ran away without a word.

I am of the belief that we learn lessons from every relationship we encounter. What did I learn from this one? I came to the understanding that there is a right way and a wrong way in doing things. I learnt the importance of communication and respect. I should have made the effort to sit and speak to him about how I felt and not run away like I was Bolt in the Olympics. My mask was getting thicker and heavier by the day. If we ignore our past and the problems that have accumulated, they can and will ruin our future. It is impossible to not deal with deep-rooted issues and just expect them to disappear. I still had not dealt with all my issues and they would continue to affect me until I did.

The Rebound That Stuck

I was working at a local grocery store and that was where I met Damien. I was fresh out of a relationship and really wasn't interested in another one. I knew Damien liked me but I never paid it any attention because like I said, I wasn't interested. Anyhow, we became friends, and the roller coaster ride began. We started to hang out and after a couple months decided to enter into a relationship. Here I was again, attempting another 'suicide'.

My virginity started to feel less of a treasure and more of a burden. I felt like it was time to just get it over with and move on, and so I did. We ended up together for about three years and it was an extremely unhealthy and unstable relationship. Don't get me wrong, we had plenty of good times, but in my opinion, the bad outweighed the good. I hope you just didn't come to the conclusion in your mind that he was the problem. If you did, then obviously you weren't listening to anything I was telling you thus far. WAKE UP!

The unhealthy person in the relationship was me. Go figure. He was one of the most caring and fun guys I had ever known, but with my cold-hearted self, I tried to suck the life out of him, literally! I was unhappy, he was happy and clearly that wasn't about to work for me. Do you really have any idea how the enemy works? Satan had me under his control, made me miserable, and used me to make everyone I came into contact with just like me.

Some medical issues I had then hindered me from being sexually active. So, not only was I going through pain emotionally, spiritually and mentally, but also physically. I would be paralyzed with pain; the doctors had no idea what was going on. Tests after tests, poking and probing, I felt drained. Talk about deception, for in my mind I felt that if he wasn't able to get the sex he wanted from me, then he would get it from someone else. That's when all the drama started.

Damien and I were together every minute of the day yet I would still accuse him of cheating. I knew in my heart he wasn't doing anything, but I just couldn't help it. Why? That's simple; the strongman was running my life. I was not in control; he was. I was a raging insecure maniac. The hulk had nothing on me. No Joke. I even turned green. In all honesty I never understood how Damien was able to stay with me that long.

If it was me I would have left me a long time ago, the truth is the truth and nothing less. I'm just being real. It's tough being in a relationship with someone who accuses you every day. All relationships should be built on trust, and without it you have nothing. It's only a matter of time before the relationship crumbles and guess what, mine did. Eventually he got tired of the accusations and decided it was time to move on. His words were, "I need a break." Well, that break lasted forever. Could I blame him, should I blame him? NO. Why should he be unhappy because I couldn't pull myself together and deal with my issues? Despite knowing that I was the cause of the break up, I was hurting, depressed and alone yet again. I felt like my world had just come to a standstill. Was I now facing the consequences for what I had done to Ray? I was furious that Damien would leave after three years and act like it meant nothing.

I had the S[**he's**] Br[**ok**]en Syndrome. I believe it's harder for women after a relationship is over because while we are broken up and emotional, men try to act like everything is ok. In reality he was hurting as he later confessed, but with him not showing he cared at the time, it really affected me. I would call and message him to see if we could work things out, but that boy was having none of it. He would ignore my calls and when he did answer, he would be extremely rude and hateful towards me. At that time I was not a party girl, but when we broke up, I found myself partying a lot in hopes of seeing him. (Stalker much.. HAHA!)

I couldn't eat, I couldn't sleep and – I wasn't able to think straight. How was I supposed to regroup after giving a part of my life to someone? I cared about this guy and he had rejected me. I was a train wreck. After being with someone for a while, it's hard to imagine yourself without them. I think what shook me up the most was the fact that he had moved on so quickly, without a thought, and was soon in another relationship with a girl who we mutually knew. I would cry every single day: at work, at school and at play. Yup, that's about right.

"How could he have said he loved me and yet leave me like that?" I would think, "Wasn't I worth fighting for?" Things happen and life goes on whether we like it or not. It's about riding the waves of life as they come. What did I learn throughout this process with Damien?

Proverbs 21:19 Better to dwell in the wilderness, than with a contentious and angry woman.

I learned the importance of not being contentious. There is nothing more annoying to a man than a bitter and angry woman. A nagging woman would be the downfall of any man. Just take a look at Samson and Delilah. I sure wasn't any Delilah in the sense; but in reality, I was very contentious and annoying. I also realized that when everything seems hopeless, there is always a light at the end of the tunnel. JESUS! Weeping may endure for the night, but joy surely does come in the morning.

Satan (laughing diabolically): I have her now!

Angel: That's what you think.

God: Hold on a little more, Princess. My strength is made perfect in your weakness.

Isaiah 41:10 Fear not, for I am with you; be not dismayed, for I am your God. I will strengthen you, Yes, I will help you, I will uphold you with my righteous right hand.

Dear Diary,

When I thought that it was the end, it just so happened that it was only the beginning. As someone once said, "Sometimes our lives have to be completely rearranged so that we can be relocated to where God wants us to be."

Chapter 3

Can Foul-mouthed Sinner be Saved?

John 3:16 *For God so loved the world that He gave His only begotten Son, that whoever believes in Him should not perish but have everlasting life.*

After my break-up with Damien I ended up someplace I never expected to be. God was about to do a new thing, something so new that I was shocked - CHURCH. On special occasions I would go with my friend Samantha who was a Christian. Having nothing to do after my breakup and with so much time on my hands, I became a frequent visitor.

Isaiah 43:19 *Behold, I will do a new thing, now it shall spring forth; shall you not know it? I will even make a road in the wilderness and rivers in the desert.*

Being in church is the best place to be after your heart has been broken. Other than God being the heart mender, it's the only place you can go and scream and bawl your eyes out and people would be ok with it. They would probably believe you were filled with the Holy Ghost or something. So instead of letting out my frustrations at home and being taken to the psychiatric hospital, I was in church screaming my lungs out and getting the release. I was not completely over Damien but being in this new atmosphere, I grew curious about this thing called Christianity.

Could I really do this? Was it even possible? Why would God want a dirty, foul-mouthed sinner like me? The more I attended church and became involved, the more bearable the pain became. Who was this Jesus and what did He want with me? After a couple of months of being curious, I just knew within my spirit that I needed this man called Jesus I had heard about.

I accepted Christ as my Savior in June 2009, and followed with water baptism. Was I even ready for this step? I hadn't a clue, but I was about to find out. Despite giving myself to God, the demons still haunted me at night. *How ugly you are! You're not worth it! You will always be rejected! Nobody wants you! Do you think Jesus loves you?* HAHAHAHA! They laughed and made fun of me. I felt as if I would never be free of these tormentors.

Satan: So He thinks it's over; He has her now, but she still has a piece of me.

My Angel: Don't give up, Shaniqua; I will fight those demons on your behalf.

God: Princess, This is just the beginning.

I was about to try this Christian thing. I wasn't perfect but I would at least give it try. I never knew what deliverance was, and so, I continued to be in bondage. I thought at times something was wrong with me, because people said when I accept Christ I would be a new creation, but I didn't feel like it. I really wanted to live right, but why did it feel as if that new creation thing I heard about skipped me? The hurt and the pain from the past were still very present and the demons still had a big influence on my life.

How could I be this new creature with these old shackles chaining me to the floor? "Was I even saved?" I asked myself. Only later did I understand that my spirit was the new creature, but I would have to deal with issues of the unsurrendered soul; I would have to battle against the enemy and take a hold of the soulish behavior.

Upon accepting Christ, our dead spirit becomes alive as the Holy Spirit comes and lives within us. However, I had to put my soul and flesh out of commission. They were ruling before I was regenerated, so now I had to constantly renew my mind and walk in the Spirit, laying aside all fleshly things. But these things I was yet to know.

I was going to church every time the doors would open, but I had no relationship with Christ. At that time, my definition of Church was about being there and participating in activities. Little did I know then that it was not about religion or activities, but all about a relationship with Him. I was trying to pick up the pieces of my heart from my shattered relationship with Damien. Despite finding this Jesus, I was still in need of and searching for love, Lo and behold, in walked Chase. Can a girl get a break?

Dear Diary,

After all, a foul-mouthed sinner can be saved. I guess a leopard can change his spots. Many things I did had changed because of the step I took, but on the other hand, many things remained the same. Was I even worthy of a relationship with Jesus? Why won't Satan just give up and leave me be? Why did it seem as if I was his target and he kept shooting at me with an AK 47?

Chapter 4

The Battle for the Soul

Luke 22:31-32 And the Lord said, "Simon, Simon! Indeed, Satan has asked for you, that he may sift you as wheat. But I have prayed for you; that your faith should not fail; and when you have returned to Me, strengthen your brethren.

Mr. Cool

Who said the enemy ever gives up? Let me introduce you to Chase, aka Mr. Cool aka the lust of the flesh. From the moment I met him, the spirits in me started to dance. You didn't know spirits attract other spirits? Well, now you do. We had the same unclean spirits residing in us and they attracted each other. We started to form a connection spiritually; it was not a godly connection by the way, but one of lust from the enemy. Should I even be entertaining another guy again? What was the harm in a little conversation?

Satan: Let's get some more demons in there.

Angel: What does it profit a man to gain the world and lose his soul?

God: Resist the devil, Princess and he shall flee from you.

I was forewarned by my friend Samantha about Chase and his player ways. Did it even matter to me? No! We as Christians have to understand how serious the spirit realm is and how deceiving the enemy can be. The spirits that resided in Chase, fed on the spirit of rejection that resided in me. Hence why I said above, the spirits in me started to dance when I met him. I had accepted Christ, but Satan was not having it. He used Chase to eventually lure me back to the kingdom of darkness.

I thank God for never letting me go even when I let go of Him. We talked, and eventually, we disclosed our feelings for each other. But then, somehow we got into an argument and everything came to a halt. We stopped all communication completely. During this time Damien started to get back in contact with me. We would secretly talk to each other at times and I started to get a sense of false hope. After a short couple of months of not speaking, Chase and I started to pick back up from where we left off; then one thing led to another.

Remember me telling you in the beginning that I'm not about to sugarcoat anything for you? Well... here we go; but before we move on, let me just say, *"I am not what I have done, but I am what I have overcome."* -Ritu Ghatourey. So when you feel the need to judge me from my past, you remember that. Did I mention his mouth was like candy? He spoke to the spirits within me and told them what they wanted to hear.

I was a goner and didn't even realize it. I was told fornication was a sin and that it was not right to be involved sexually; I was given instructions not to do something, without an explanation as to why. It didn't make any sense to me as a new convert with a sexual past. I knew what sex was like and now someone was telling me I had to stop? Are you serious? We are all curious beings. Have you ever realized when there's a wet paint sign saying "Don't touch; WET PAINT", people still tend to touch out of curiosity? Well, that's me. Why would this Jesus not want me to have sex? What's the big deal anyway? Did He not know how great sex was? Why did He want me to stop? I was not given biblical understanding on why it was necessary to live pure before God. And so, curiosity killed the cat.

I was walking and holding hands with God but winking at the Devil. It was a love affair and I was in deep. I was dealing with them both and nobody wanted to give me up. Moreover, I didn't want to let them go. I wanted to gain the pleasure but still expected to serve God. I had two masters and this was wrong. God wanted me, but I refused to let go of Satan. Someone once said, "The bridge is just the way from one kingdom to the other;" I could not stay on it and I needed to cross over, but I wouldn't. I refused to cross over on either side so I stayed holding strong onto that bridge.

Matthew 6:24 No one can serve two masters; for either he will hate the one and love the other, or else he will be loyal to the one and despise the other. You cannot serve God and mammon.

Chase and I eventually started to have sex. Did I just say sex? **YES**. It's so funny how the church is gravely afraid of the three-letter word SEX. I guess mouths just dropped open; close your mouth, it's still open by the way. Can I shock you again? In all honesty, can I add that I was also now again sexually active with Damien? How did that happen you ask? My heart was split in four, God, Satan, Damien and Chase.

I was familiar with Damien for so long that when he came back I fell prey to his attention. I used Chase as a means to get over him and that I did after a while. In the meantime, however, I was basically giving myself to two men at the same time. YES, honey! I was in church giving God those praises, or should I say half praises and sexing with the devil. Sex is from God but the perversion of sex is from the enemy.

I was now in church, involved with ministry and sexing like I didn't have a care in the world. I was getting my freak on and then going to church on Sundays. Hypocrite much? I did not fully understand this Jesus thing and so being involved in sexual sin meant nothing to me. Damien and I decided to call it quits; after all he was using me, wasn't he?

He was in a relationship with someone else but at random times, he would message or call me. Sounds familiar? Note that these were mostly night calls, so you do the math. We were both trying to cling to what we knew; he was using me, and I was allowing myself to be used. After he finally went along, my focus was solely on Chase. Desperate people do desperate things and honneyyyy, I was desperate for love. It's called, looking for love in all the wrong places.

I was having sex on Saturdays with Chase and coming to church on Sundays and acting like the biggest Christian ever. I remember one Christmas Eve being with him; we stayed with each other until four in the morning Christmas day, having church in the next hour, five o'clock. I was in love, or so

I thought; how wrong I was. Do you know sin feels sweet until you get burned? Well, sweetheart, I got first-degree burns.

I'm allergic to pineapple but does that stop me? No. I just make sure I have an antihistamine around. Can something be bad for you and you still entertain it? We do this all the time. Sin feels good when you're in the act, but the consequences, regret and guilt that come after, leave you sick. Is it then worth it? If you know that person or thing in your life is bad for you, then why are you still entertaining it?

I had a deep desire to enter another relationship. I was allowing loneliness to get the best of me. I was not concerned with the fact that Chase was not walking in the will of God; I just wanted and needed to feel as if someone wanted me. I then found out that Chase was talking to someone else and this was the person to whom he gave the title "girlfriend". By the way, she was within our circle and I didn't know until I was already in deep.

It would hurt to see them together, knowing all the things he would say to me. Both these guys had used me at their disposal. So where did this leave me? I was the booty call, maybe a high-class prostitute who did not get paid very well. Can I even say that? I hope that I won't be thrown out from the church after this confession. I did tell you guys I would not sugarcoat anything. I was hurt, annoyed and angry, but that didn't last for too long because before you knew it, I was back in his arms.

I continued to see him despite knowing he was with someone else. I felt like I was there first so she needed to go. Isn't it amazing the things you put up with when you're afflicted with low self-worth? When you believe you're not good enough, you can find yourself settling for less than you deserve. I was willing to settle for mere crumbs that would drop from the table, believing I wasn't deserving of the feast.

That old sneaky serpent had me so blinded to the truth that I began to grow animosity in my heart for a girl who didn't even know what we were doing. My morals were compromised; what I believed in, no longer mattered. I was blinded tremendously by the enemy and his spirits. I was one who had always detested cheating and here I was, still involved with this guy after finding out that he was with someone else. Rejected people crave attention and acceptance, even if there is a compromise to get it, they will. After a time of going to church, something new started to happen - CONVICTION. I found that I started to feel grieved in my spirit; I could no longer raise my hands and sing or say amen. I was now uncomfortable. Instead of feeling angry towards this girl, I started to feel sad, compassion, hurt and the list goes on. My heart began to melt day after day, conviction and guilt started to penetrate my soul and spirit. "I can't do this anymore!" I screamed. I told him to make a choice and so he did; he chose her.

At what point would this rejection stop? Was something wrong with me? Wasn't I good enough? Couldn't anybody see my worth and choose me for once? I was just used and discarded like a piece of old dirty tissue. Yes, I felt that bad. I asked questions, questions and more questions, while the tears began to trickle down. I felt cheap and worthless, I had basically prostituted myself for love and it still didn't work. I used my body to try to get what I wanted and it wasn't successful. Was I that unlovable? What was wrong with me that everyone kept leaving?

I remember going to church one night and a prophet was preaching. He gave an altar call and I was literally shaking like crazy. I knew I had to go up, but I couldn't move because I was afraid that he would call me out in my fornication and the whole church would know. We are so caught up believing that a prophet will tell our business, when all the while, we miss the Word God has for us. While I was thinking about being ratted out, I heard him say from the pulpit, "God is not in the business of making anyone shame, so to that person, God is saying come now."

I remember taking that step that night, feet shaking, hands sweating, but I made it to the altar. God spoke to me about every single thing that I was doing. Just as the prophet said, He did not cause me shame that night, but revealed my wrong doings to me only. I cried like a baby and made a pledge to God that night about my purity. I made a vow to be abstinent until marriage, and that is a vow I will definitely not be breaking.

When we fornicate, it creates ungodly soul ties. We are tying ourselves to that person in an ungodly way. It is said that when the male makes a deposit in the female, he leaves a piece of himself spiritually. And we wonder why we can't seem to get over that person. An ungodly soul tie is explained as the spiritual connection of one person's soul to another person's soul. We create an invisible bond to another human being. Every time we have sexual intercourse with someone, we become one flesh with that person. You are knitted to that person in every way possible. This is why in the Word it says, "...and the two shall become one flesh". This also means sexually. See then why it's so hard to shake them?

I had now become one flesh with two people, but was that even possible? This is why God places the importance of purity and saving ourselves for marriage. Your spirit, emotions, every aspect of your being is knitted to that person. We often believe that God is holding us back from something but in reality, He is saving us from much heartache and pain. Abstinence is God's only protection policy when it comes to sex before marriage. We should have a desire to live pure before God, giving Him our bodies as a living sacrifice. Look at it this way. Jesus gave His body as a sacrifice for you, so why can't you give your body as a sacrifice unto Him.

1 Corinthians 6:18-20 Flee sexual immorality. Every sin that a man does is outside the body, but he who commits sexual immorality sins against his own body. Or do you not know that your body is the temple of the Holy Spirit who is in you, whom you have from God, and you are not your own? For you were bought at a price; therefore glorify God in your body and in your spirit, which are God's.

I want to stop here for a moment and take some time as Juanita Bynum did in her book "No more Sheets" to apologize to a sister in Christ. To you my sister, the one I had a hand in causing great pain, I am truly sorry. I want to apologize publically to you despite my horrible actions were in private. We are sisters and I should have been woman enough to walk away from the situation and not cause you pain. I know you have forgiven me as I have also forgiven myself and I am thankful. I will never again allow myself be blinded by the enemy and hurt another sister again.

To anyone who might be reading this and have found themselves in a situation with another person's spouse, you need to STOP. It may be funny to you because you have that woman's man, but it won't be funny when someone else comes and takes him away from both of you. I don't believe in karma, but I do believe in consequences for your actions. Whatever a man sows that he shall indeed reap. If he is cheating with you, be sure that he will cheat on you when you finally get him. We have to look out for each other as women.

If he really loved you, then he wouldn't be confused about who he wants to be with. You may be laughing now and think she is the joke, but if you don't quit while you are ahead, you my dear, will be the joke. My aim is to stop you from making the same mistakes I have made, and not fall into the traps that I fell into. BABY GIRL, STOP being that man's booty call.

Dear Diary,

Despite the devastating pain that Chase caused me, I learnt the importance of purity. I have come to the understanding that in every negative there is a positive. The enemy wanted to bring destruction but God used it to the benefit of my destiny. I may have fallen, but now I have the opportunity to catch someone before they hit the ground. My mistakes will be used to strengthen my brethren. Satan wanted to sift me, but Jesus interceded on my behalf. My failures are now a testimony.

Chapter 5

Where Do I go From Here?

Galatians 5:17 *For the flesh lusts against the Spirit and the Spirit against the flesh; and these are contrary to one another, so that you do not do the things that you wish.*

Satan: I'm not letting her go.

God: Neither will I.

I was now tied up with two people emotionally, mentally and spiritually. How could I get rid of these soul ties, strongholds and spirits that were intruding in my life? I had now added baggage on top of the ones I already had. It was like adding insult to injury. Every step I took, I was making the situation worse. I gave the demons more to feed on. I came into revelation of having a relationship with the Lord and not just coming to church. I loved God and wanted to serve Him faithfully with all my heart, but where was I to start? It was hard.

"You're looking for love in all the wrong places," He said. "The only one who can truly satisfy the human heart is the One who made it, and that's Me." I was more depressed than ever and I had a very hard time accepting the forgiveness God wanted to extend towards me. He had already forgiven me, but I couldn't forgive myself. I was battling with what I had done, and the pain I had inflicted on this girl's life. There are no words to describe how I felt at that time. Whenever I would convince myself that God had forgiven me, the enemy would bring back up my past.

Romans 8:1 There is therefore now no condemnation to those who are in Christ Jesus, who do not walk according to the flesh, but according to the Spirit.

There was condemnation alright, but it was coming from Satan. The guilt started to eat me alive. He would consistently tell me that I wasn't good enough and that God didn't want anything to do with me anymore; I could as well come back to him. I would cry so much, day after day, minute after minute. I was like the prodigal son in **Luke 15:11-32.** While God wanted to restore me to the full dignity of sonship, I kept insisting on settling to be a hired servant.

I felt worthless. It is sometimes extremely hard for us to receive God's forgiveness. We hold onto our sin, when God wants to erase our past and offer us a new beginning. I thought that my sin and shame were too much for God to forgive. How could a holy God forgive me of such a sin like that?

Luke 15: 17-19 But when he came to himself, he said, 'How many of my father's hired servants have bread enough and to spare, and I perish with hunger! I will arise and go to my father, and will say to Him, "Father, I have sinned against heaven and before you, and I am no longer worthy to be called your son. Make me like one of your hired servants.

Just like the son, I was ready to settle for less because my mentality was messed up in the pig pen. I was filthy and defiled; I came from a place where I didn't think it was possible to become a son again. I saw myself as damaged goods. I was about to accept the contract the son wanted, which was to become a servant and not the one the father wanted to give him, which was his sonship back. Like the father of the prodigal son, God looked at me in all of my muck, hugged me and welcomed me back home. He wanted to restore me to full sonship, but I could not accept it. I figured my sin was so hideous, that I rightfully deserved to be a hired servant. "I had committed the worst sin ever," I thought to myself. "He wouldn't want me back as a son."

Luke 15: 20-24 And he arose and came to his father. But when he was still a great way off, his father saw him and had compassion, and ran and fell on his neck and kissed him. And the son said to him, "Father, I have sinned against heaven and in your sight, and am no longer worthy to be call your son". But the father said to his servants, "Bring out the best robe and put it on him, and put a ring on his hand and sandals on his feet. And bring the fatted calf here and kill it, and let us eat and be merry; for this my son was dead and is alive again; he was lost and is found." And they began to be merry.

Reading the text, we see how happy the father was at his son's return. He ran out to greet him, not interested in his past or what he had done. Nor did he give him a long lecture about where he had been or who he had been with. The father was just filled with joy to see his son and was not interested about the sins of his past. He then forgave the son and accepted him back into fellowship, refusing to bring him on as a hired hand and welcomed him as his son, with full rights restored. I was covered in the filth that I had accumulated from being in the pig pen with Damien and Chase, but God looked past my mistakes and welcomed me back into His loving embrace as a son and not a servant. My muck didn't bother Him at all, but it was surely bothering me.

His daughter was lost and now was found and for that He began to celebrate. God took away my filthy clothes and covered me in the robe of righteousness; He placed the ring on my finger and sandals on my feet. He brought out the fatted calf and decided to throw a party for His daughter. He wanted me to see myself the way He saw me. No more shame and disgrace, but the position of rightful heir. To Him, I was like a lily among thorns, the apple of His eye, but I was just not seeing what My Daddy saw. Another story which shows restoration and forgiveness is found in the book of Zechariah with Joshua the High Priest.

Zechariah 3: 1-5 Then he showed me Joshua the high priest standing before the Angel of the Lord, and Satan standing at his right hand to oppose him. And the Lord said to Satan, "The Lord rebuke you, Satan! The Lord who has chosen Jerusalem rebuke you! Is this not a brand plucked from the fire?" Now Joshua was clothed with filthy garments, and was standing before the Angel. Then He answered and spoke to those who stood before Him, saying, "Take away the filthy garments from him" And to him

He said, "See, I have removed your iniquity from you, and I will clothe you with rich robes." And I said, "Let them put a clean turban on his head." So they put a clean turban on his head, and they put the clothes on him. And the Angel of the Lord stood by.

Joshua stood before God in sin, probably full of shame like I was, feeling disgusted and undeserving. Satan also stood before God ready to condemn Joshua, but the Lord immediately said to Satan, "The Lord rebuke you." Watch My Daddy putting the devil in his place. There is a quote that says, "Satan knows you name but he calls you by your sin; God knows your sin but He calls you by your name."

The devil was ready to call out Joshua, just as he was calling me out in my sin, he was ready to contest, but God was not having it, not one bit of it. Joshua, like me and the prodigal son, was stripped of his filthy clothes and clothed with rich garments. God had forgiven us; He took away our iniquity, just as if we had never sinned, but it was up to us to accept that forgiveness. If you are reading this book and have found yourself in the position of the prodigal son, I urge you to find your way back home and accept the forgiveness of your Father. You are never too far gone that God won't accept you back.

At this moment, your sin may seem too great to be forgiven, but I want you to know that God wants to heal and restore you to rightful sonship. He is waiting with loving arms, spread open for the moment you walk through the door. Stop listening to the lies of the enemy and the guilt he has burdened you with. God can take away your filthy rags and replace them with rich garments. God is the restorer. Reconciliation is right at hand if you are only willing to forgive yourself and accept the forgiveness of God.

Your father is awaiting your arrival my dear child; come on home. You have strayed for too long, the appointed time is NOW. God is not interested in how big you believe your sin is, He just wants you to return home that He can love up on you. Daddy is waiting, baby girl!

1 John 1:9 If we confess our sins, He is faithful and just to forgive us our sins and to cleanse us from all unrighteousness.

I was still fighting many demons, but I was not about to let them take me down without a fight. I made the decision to stop playing church and become the Christian I ought to be. The flesh and the spirit were at war, and it was up to me to determine who would win. I began to starve my flesh with the Word of God and began to acquire a hunger and thirst for the Lord. I made the decision to starve my distractions and feed my focus.

What did I learn from this experience? I was able to understand the importance of purity and the effects of sex outside of marriage. To know that it is never my job to force someone to love me, and that not everyone you lose is a loss. That you should never keep giving what you're not getting, because love is not one sided.

I still suffered from my rejection and insecurities, but I was not about to wallow in self-pity and let my flesh win this battle. I was ready to go hard for Christ. I never thought that I would have fallen in love when I first started out this Jesus thing, but I did, so I was ready to fight. I had finally found the Man who wouldn't break my heart. His name was Jesus, the greatest love story ever told.

Newness

> **Romans 8:28** *And we know that all things work together for good to those who love God, to those who are the called according to His purpose.*

I had made the decision to live right before God and be the person He had called me to be. It sounds very easy, but for a person who was still suffering from deep rooted issues, it was at times quite hard. In 2011, God had spoken to me about attending bible school. "This is a joke," I told Him. I had never thought about bible school and was not at all interested. After some procrastination and confirmation, I decided it was best if I didn't disobey and end up in the belly of a great fish.

I was not about to play with God. I would not look cute in the belly of some fish. This was a big step for me because I did not know how I was about to pay for school seeing that I only worked two days a week and had bills to pay. I made the decision to trust God and place everything in His hands. I have learnt that God will not call you without equipping and providing for you. I had to place my unknown future in the hands of an all-knowing God and that I decided to do.

I started my journey at the West Indies School of Theology in September 2011 and despite not knowing the reason for being there, I was excited because I knew God had sent me; I just didn't know why. My walk with Christ was beginning to bloom. I was in a class with people who were on fire for Christ and it showed. Being around them had given me a greater desire to further my relationship with God. Everything was going good, I had forgotten about Chase and my main focus was on Christ. I thought. I had dealt with my rejection and insecurities, so I kept my head in the Word and my books. Then, Jordan came along. Seriously! Was God about to play me again? Truth is, I was about to play myself.

Dear Diary,

I have learnt that serving God doesn't mean you won't have difficulties or struggles. You will have to fight some battles, but you won't have to fight alone. In our difficult moments we should tag God, He's always waiting to come to our rescue.

Chapter 6

Where Did You Come From?

Jordan was like the story that was told when you were younger, about the stork bringing the baby and dropping it at your doorstep. The baby came out of nowhere and so did he. I was out with my friends one night and Alyssa happened to see a guy she knew. He came over and started having a conversation with us. He was talking about his friend being in the car sleeping and so Samantha and I told him to go get him. Had I just made a mistake? Let's find out. Eventually he came and sat with us and we all got into conversation. Jordan seemed like a pretty cool guy. He was a Christian for one. √ Check. Yes, I was checking those boxes. I know you girls do it too, so quit fronting. He was funny and by his answers to questions thrown at him, it seemed as if he knew his Bible.

Now ladies, just because a guy say he's a Christian, doesn't mean he has a relationship with God. I am one for asking random questions about things in the Bible I believe you should know, but wouldn't know if you don't read. Got that? I won't ask you about David, Jonah, Moses and Samson. These are all stories from Sunday School and I'm not your Sunday School teacher. My goal is to find out if you use that Bible as a prop or if you actually read it. About two weeks after that day, we started talking on the phone through messaging. I had never met a person who completely wanted everything I wanted out of life as I did; or so it seemed. It was really weird the way we wanted the same things, from the amount of children, right down to morals and values and even the type of house.

We would talk for countless hours throughout the night about God and discuss the Bible. I am the girl who is up at 1:00 in the morning ready to discuss the Word of God and get some study on. It seemed like everything was on the green light. He was a Christian, fun, liked a good laugh, seemed to know his Bible and wanted the same things I did. I asked God countless times to direct me and show me if this was the person for me or not. He said YES; or did He? I thought I was hearing clearly, but I guess I wasn't. I remember receiving a prophecy around the time Jordan and I had begun talking, and the prophetess said, "God has nothing but the best for you." I took that as confirmation that this was His best for me. Boy!! Was I wrong.

We have to understand that Satan is a sly old fox. Remember that song you learnt in Sunday School? Yes, if only we could put him in a box and throw away the key, all our problems would be over. The only truth to that song is that Satan is indeed a sly fox! Not going to sing it for you now, but he loves to do a counterfeit of the original. He performs miracles as well. We see that in the Bible with Simon the sorcerer.

Acts 8:9-10 But there was a certain man called Simon, who previously practiced sorcery in the city and astonished the people

*of Samaria, claiming that he was someone great, to whom they
all gave heed, from the least to the greatest, saying, This man is
the great power of God.*

My mind was set; I had heard God loud and clear and this was the one. Notwithstanding my thoughts, I still prayed to God and said, "Lord, if Jordan is not your best for me shake things up and remove him from my life." If I was so sure he was the one why did I pray such a thing? Beats me! We were getting to know each other and everything was going cool until one day I messaged Jordan and he didn't reply. I didn't think anything much of it because I knew he was tired from work and so the next day I anticipated a call or message. That call or message never came and so I proceeded to message him to see what was up.

Little did I know I was in for a shocker. I will forever remember everything that was said to me in those messages that day. He told me he needed space and time to pray and consult God. Now, that was ok with me because I am all for guidance from Daddy God. However, what he went on to say was what scorched my soul. "You have no drive; I would date you and have you as a girlfriend but you're not a person I would marry."

Talk about burn. Apply cold water to burn area. Quick!! (HAHA) The words he said did more damage than the fact that he rejected me. Yes, I was hurt by the fact that he didn't want to be with me, but the words cut deeper. I would really like to meet the person who came up with the statement, "Sticks and stones may break my bones but words will never hurt me." Words hurt and they have the power to break you worse than physical pain.

As I continue, you remember what I had said to God? "If Jordan isn't your best for me, then remove him from my life." The things I thought I had dealt with were now back and rearing their ugly heads. I felt really broken and depressed about two things: the fact that he made me feel insignificant and on top of that, low with his words. "I would date you, but you're not someone I would marry." If I wasn't wife material, then what was I?

The other thing that completely shook me was me questioning if I was really a sheep. I thought I had heard from God and I didn't. I cried out, "God if I didn't hear your voice, then whose voice did I hear? If you said your sheep know Your voice and I didn't hear correctly, does it mean I am not a sheep but a goat?" Not being able to distinguish my Daddy's voice crippled me.

John 10:27 My sheep hear My voice, and I know them, and they follow Me.

Demon: You will never get away from me, I have been sent with a mission.

God: He who dwells in the secret place of the Most High, shall abide under the shadow of the Almighty. I am Your refuge and strength.

Dear Diary,

My soul is rattled at the thought of being a goat. As a sheep in the flock I ought to be hearing my Shepherd's voice. Shouldn't I? My desire is to be broken and stripped of anything that isn't of God. My urgency for freedom has just escalated to a newer level. I am desperate for wholeness in my life. Where do I start?

Chapter 7

Brokenness

Psalm 51:17 The sacrifices of God are a broken spirit, a broken and a contrite heart, these, O God, You will not despise.

Brokenness is a part of the process that must happen before God is able to put the pieces back together. Through this brokenness is where wholeness will be established. God was about to strip me like never before and I knew it. I was frustrated and tired of this feeling of unworthiness and I needed God to work a miracle for me. This was about me and God and not about me and Jordan. I screamed and cried out to God repeatedly night and day and asked Him to break me. Was I ready for it? We ought to be careful what we ask for because we sure will get it.

An egg cannot be used unless it's broken, and God was about to break me so that He could use me. I sought after God like never before, and kept begging him to strip me of the demons that were tormenting me. In this alone time with Him, so much was revealed to me and I was able to understand a lot more. He said once again, "Why are you looking for love in all the wrong places, Princess? The only one who can truly satisfy your heart is Me." He proceeded to show me that while I was seeking the attention of man, He was waiting for me to seek Him wholeheartedly. He wanted me to completely surrender myself to Him and allow Him to fight my battles.

In spite of me being in bible school and going hard for Christ, I had never surrendered my all. There is a song by William McDowell that says, "I surrender all to You, Everything I give to You, Withholding nothing." That was definitely not me. I was robbing God and He of all people did not deserve it. It was easy for me to let go of Jordan, but it was extremely hard for me to accept that I made a mistake about the voice of my Daddy. Being able to distinguish my Father's voice is very important to me and should be for any believer.

I found myself crying every minute, but it was not a cry of sadness or happiness, it was a cry that said I had enough and I wanted out. It was a cry that was saying, "God this is the last straw, I've been crippled for twenty-six years too long." For some time I went into prayer and fasting, and I remember Friday being my last day. My fast would go from 6:00 am − 6:00 pm; I had church that same night at 7:30. When I got home from work that day, God spoke to me loudly and told me not to let a drop of food touch my mouth until He said. He further instructed me to get my olive oil and anoint my entire body and keep praying and praising Him.

I remember going to church that night knowing within my spirit that something was about to happen. At church everything was running smoothly and everyone broke out in prayer and worship. I recall talking to myself and saying, "God, I am not going back home like this, You have to do something." I paced back and forth like a crazy person in the pew quietly repeating myself. My pastor decided to give an altar call and it turned out to be the break I needed for my deliverance. What was this call about? If I told you I remember I would be lying, all I can recount from that night was that I needed to be at the altar.

I found my way to the altar and that was the beginning of my stripping. Talk about crying, bawling, screaming, the snotty nose, I did it all. I needed a release and I was not about to be worried about who was watching. This was between me and my Daddy and things needed to be set in order. The beginning of my deliverance process started that night and it felt great. God was waiting on me for so long to move out of my place of slumber. I had been prophesied over many times about what God had in store for my life. I was also given the gift of dreams and through them God would speak to me and show me the great things I was destined to accomplish. I started to act a little bit like Jonah and tried to run away from God. It was scary for me to believe the things that God would show me and I would dismiss everything and be lazy. "God!" I exclaimed, "But why me? Not me surely! Are you sure you want me? Isn't there anyone else you can use? Are you sure you have the right person?" That was my cry many times.

God was calling me out for so long and I was constantly procrastinating. In my opinion I was not worthy enough to be that person He was calling me to be. We have to stop with all the complaints and get up from our laziness and know that if God calls us we must obey. We have to understand that obedience is better than sacrifice. At some point we all make the mistake of trying to run from God and doing what we want to without much concern about what He wants. But I'm convinced that in spite of our falling short, something good will come out of it. Jonah ran from God because he did not want to do the task that was assigned to him. Guess what? Because of his Olympic running skills, a ship full of men rejected their gods and turned to the one true God.

We may change the plans because of our stubbornness, but the purpose of God will not be thwarted. Not only did the people of Nineveh repent, but the men on the ship did as well. God used the disobedience of Jonah to change the hearts of those men. We may run away from God saying, "What if I fail?" But God is saying, "What if you fly?" I had known rejection all my life, but I was never aware of how to handle it. Charles Swindoll said, *"Life is 10 percent what happens to you and 90 percent of how you react to it."* Rejection is a part of life that everyone will encounter at some point. The way we deal with that rejection will determine how we live our lives. In order for me to move on from the past, I had to finally deal with 26 years of pent up rejection and hurt.

I had spent years wondering what was wrong with me, and what I could do differently that I wouldn't be rejected again. I often felt worthless, not being able to see my worth and wondered if anyone would ever see it. For everyone who came into my life, I would always await their exit. I would always sit and tap my foot and wonder how long it would take them to leave. I was so used to people giving up and letting me go, I naturally expected it to happen and looked forward to it. The devil had spent years training me, molding and shaping me into the woman he wanted. I have come to the realization that rejection doesn't mean that you're not good enough; it basically means that the other person was not wise enough to notice what you brought to the table, and that's ok.

It's about learning how to accept it, and moving on. Whenever someone rejects you, it's their failure to not see your worth. However, it's your job to not let that rejection rule you and make you bitter. Lena Horne said, "It's not the load that breaks you down, it's the way you carry it." When people forsake you, turn to God, for He will take care of you.

Psalm 27:10 *When my father and my mother forsake me, then the Lord will take care of me.*

God continued to speak to me and gave me insight on how to deal with my issues. I made the decision to look into the mirror ever so often and compliment myself instead of being my own worst critic. It's not the easiest thing to have to look in the mirror and see a face each day that you don't love. How could anyone begin to love me if I didn't first love myself? I had spent years of believing I was ugly and unworthy, so I had to change my mindset. I had to come into an understanding of the love God had for me and to see myself the way He saw me.

I had to stop letting Satan contaminate my spirit and feed my soul garbage. I was loved and cherished; fearfully and wonderfully made in the image of my Creator and I had to let that soak into my mind. He took His time and formed and fashioned me into the person I am. Every single detail He took into consideration, so who am I to say that I am ugly. Loving me was a journey and I was ready to take the ride. It was not going to be easy but it was indeed necessary. I hadn't made a mistake of sending for Jordan out of the car that night, for to-date we are good friends and both of us are over what happened. The mistake I made was trying to force something out of nothing. He came into my life for a reason and it was not that of a husband-wife relationship, but a good friendship.

Dear Diary,

Brokenness doesn't mean that it's over; it is said that broken crayons still color. Anything that is broken can be made whole and used again when God has anything to do with it. In Acts chapter 27, Paul was involved in a shipwreck. The ship was destroyed as forewarned by God but the broken parts of the ship were used to get some of the people safely to shore. It didn't matter how broken I thought I was, My Daddy has a way of using us at our worse and having something amazing spring forth. With the broken pieces in His hands, God can make the impossible, possible.

Chapter 8

Schools Out: What's Next?

Jeremiah 29:11 *For I know the thoughts that I think toward you, says the Lord, thoughts of peace and not of evil, to give you a future and a hope.*

A year had passed after that chapter with Jordan and my three years at bible school were soon going to be over. Throughout that year, I experienced the loss of the man who helped raise me and was like a grandfather. He was one of the people in my life, who, despite not being blood related, stuck by me and never left until death. This was very hard for me to deal with, but I bottled it up and continued with my studies. God had ordered my steps towards applying for school for whatever unknown reason, but what was I supposed to do when it was over? I was clueless about what my next step was going to be and the enemy wasn't making it any easier. Every angle I turned, he was trying to take me out or confuse me with his lies.

I remember becoming ill towards the end of my last term; out of nowhere, I began to experience dreadful headaches and dizzy spells. My head would hurt so much to the point where I would literally just sit and cry for several days. No matter how many doctors I visited, no one could figure out what was going on with me. Every checkup they did, the results were that I was perfectly ok. I was home for three consecutive weeks not going to church, school or work. My headaches became more intense and I had no idea where they were coming from. Needless to say, despite my illness, I still needed to make sure all my assignments were in and I was ready for my final exams. How I felt physically didn't matter; I had to push through to get the work done and I did just that. Then suddenly, out of nowhere, exams were finished and the illness was gone. Sounds crazy, huh? Not really. God had shown me that it was nothing but the devil at work. I ignored Satan's tactics and continued to prepare for graduation.

The day before graduation I went to get my hair done. Let me tell you, Satan was not about to leave me alone. For some reason he was trying his best to stop me from walking across that stage and receiving my diploma, but God was not about to have that. As I was waiting to get my hair done, all I remember was hearing my friend shouting in fear. By the time I realized what was happening, it was too late. A mirror which was about three feet in height came crashing down on my head. Looking back on that day all I can say is, "But God!" The enemy had a plan, "But God!!" I am normally a person who would panic very quickly in a situation like that, but it was miraculous to me the way I reacted. While my friend was screaming and frantic, I was extremely calm and relaxed. A three foot mirror had just come crashing down on my head, breaking into pieces and I was so relaxed, it scared me.

It was nothing other than my Daddy God that did it all. When I looked at the mirror while she was removing the fragments from my head and my body, I sat there in amazement that I only had a badly sliced finger and a few scrapes. This could have ended worse; the enemy could have won that day, but God had and has a plan for my life. With a well-bandaged finger I walked across that stage and received my diploma the next day. God had won, like He always does. After the excitement of graduation was over, I started to feel somewhat depressed and stressed. I was going through the motions about a guy called Brad (more on this later), and the question that was on everyone's lips, "So what's the next step?" was foremost in my mind.

It is tough when you don't know what the next step is, then to have people asking you what you don't know. I began to grow frustrated and stayed away from church for a while. I wanted to be alone and not have people constantly ask me a question I didn't know how to answer. Everybody thought they knew what was best for me; they all had their opinions and I was just screaming in my head for them to shut up and leave me alone. I felt like a failure. I was 28, soon about to be 29, dependent on my earthly father and I had not accomplished half of the goals I had set. I didn't have a home of my own, a proper job, a car and the list goes on.

There I was looking at my life from the world's perspective of success rather than what God wanted me to do and where He wanted me to be. The enemy wanted to cloud my judgment;

he wanted to keep me from hearing the voice of God. I understood my purpose, but I didn't know the steps to take in order to get there. God does not show us the whole picture all of the time. He expects us to trust Him and believe that He will lead us. Often times we make our own plans, but what we have to understand is that He is the one who orders our steps. It is then up to us to trust an unknown future in the hands of an all-knowing God. I had to let him take the lead, sit in the background, and ride the waves of the life He was about to take me on.

God had a plan and purpose for this life of mine, and I had to believe in Him to accomplish all that He had said. I got back into church after a couple weeks of being home wallowing in self-pity as the enemy wanted, and was on my way to fulfilling my purpose. Just like Moses, I had a moment of weakness of the flesh, but I eventually got back up and got back on track. I had work to do and I was not about to let the enemy hinder me from what God had in store for my life. Sometimes the only way God can get us to listen is if He puts us in isolation.

Dear Diary,

For a quick second I was lost, but heyyyyyy there, I'm back and ready to go. I got caught up with the success of man, forgetting that my purpose is what was important. School was over but my studying was only now about to begin. I thank God for being my Protector when the enemy wanted to take me out. He was my help in time of trouble, my shield in defense of Satan's tactics, and in the end, I came out victorious.

Chapter 9

Mc Dreamy?

I had never experienced a crush until I met Brad aka McDreamy. I had been admiring him from afar for a long while and didn't have the courage to say a thing. When I say 'a thing', I literally mean a thing. Despite my past insecurities, I was never one to be nervous around a guy but with him I was. Whenever I saw him, my palms got sweaty and my cheeks started to turn red, if that was even possible; I'm seriously dark. When he was in my presence, I would go pretty quickly from the most talkative person into this silent zone.

If it appeared that he was about to even walk in my direction, I would turn away and search for the nearest exit. Really, you ask? Yes, really! At times I would choke to even say "hi." He was handsome but he also intrigued me. Listening to him in discussions made me curious; I wondered what it would be like to get to know him. He was one mysterious individual. He had beautiful eyes - the kind you would get lost in, and I guess I did. So I decided to suck it up, and take the risk of going from completely not talking to this guy, to telling him that I liked him. I started to form random conversations with him, after all those timesn of not saying anything at all. Eventually I decided it was time for me to drop the big "I like you" bomb, and so I did. During the last couple of months of finishing school, we started talking. We became friends and decided we'd get to know each other as time progressed and see what happened.

"Isn't she tired of getting hurt?" you're probably asking. Well, I guess not. I still had some trust issues with God stemming from the scenario with Jordan. I was somewhat skeptical about the voice of God and putting it to the test was a bit challenging for me. We should never go into a potential relationship without first consulting God. Our emotions should always take a backseat to the will of God, and this is where I went wrong. I decided not to consult My Daddy on the matter and went ahead into this friendship based on the feelings I had for Brad. My emotions were taking precedence in the situation and this is why I fell flat on my face once again.

Getting caught up with Brad took me on an emotional ride, revealing that I still had some things I needed to lay aside for good. One minute he would be cool, we would hang out and have a good time, and the next minute he would become very distant and extremely cold. Up to this day he never ever actually said he liked me or that he wanted to be with me. He knew that I liked him, but he never expressed any feelings towards me. When a guy is playing Hide-and -seek with you baby girl, please let him win. You have no time to play games; your heart is at stake. If he keeps hiding, why should you keep chasing him?

That should have been my cue to leave him alone and move on, but as I said, my flesh was ruling the spirit man; my emotions were leading and not the Spirit of God. My soul baggage plus his soul baggage were causing a lot of problems. You should never hand your heart to someone who is still picking up the pieces of their own heart. I tried countless times to understand why he acted the way he did; it played on my mind. Did he even care at all? After all, he never verbally said he did. Was I just someone to pass time with until he found someone?

In his distant times he never messaged me; I was the one who did all the messaging and when he did answer, he was sharp and short. I felt like I was a dentist pulling teeth - those strong ones that refuse to come out. I would find myself making up excuses for his ways and continued to press on hoping that things would change. I remember one night he messaged me saying, "Consider us 'just friends' and nothing more!" I should have run for the hills then, right? But NAH! I didn't; I was a sucker for punishment. After a period of no contact, we started talking again and would hang out once more. We were just friends. But what is 'just friends?' He had said to consider us just friends, but when he was in his 'good' moods, he would kiss me and act like he was interested. We ought to make sure that the feelings are mutual or we'll end up pretty disappointed. Friends don't deserve any kind of marriage benefits. I was messing up my heart in the process of trying to figure out if he cared.

I was really 'in like', and so it didn't matter if he said it or not. He was not the one to blame but I was. I allowed him to touch me physically and emotionally without any commitment.

I was the one who decided to get attached to a man who didn't even make it clear if he liked me or not. He didn't waste my time, I wasted my own time. Why did I keep finding myself over and over with the same type of guy? If you want to break the cycle, stop and ask yourself, "What is wrong with me?" I remember crying to God, as usual. I think by now you will realize that I am a very emotional person. God made me that way, so just leave me alone, okay? (smile)

I asked Him what was on me that I constantly kept attracting these guys who would leave me high and dry; would play with me but would never want me. I recall one day in His presence, soaking my body in olive oil and praying while walking around like an insane person. I would chant, "God remove anything on me that keeps attracting this type of man! God remove anything on me that keeps attracting this type of man!" I surely wasn't ready for the answer. He simply said, "It's you, baby girl." I was like, "Say what now?"

God really knows how to burst your bubble, doesn't He? All the while a part of me kept blaming these guys but 'I' was the problem. If you keep going into a relationship or 'friendship', one after the next with the same issues, then it's time to check yourself. I craved his attention so much that I was willing to settle for less than I deserved. When I talked to him about how I felt with him being distant or just ignoring me, he would say, "That's just me." I felt I was too emotional or wanted too much attention, but this was not the case. The 'wrong' person will have you believing that you're asking for too much. He made me begin to believe that I wasn't worth a phone call or a message. I don't care how busy a person is or how much they don't utilize their phone, when you like someone, you will find the time to at least say "hello".

I really liked this guy but I had to get it stuck in my head that maybe he didn't feel the same way. I was the one doing the pursuing; being a hunter not knowing how to hunt. Men are hunters by nature and go after who and what they want. If he isn't making an effort to make you feel cared for, then honey, you need to stop. You should never have to play the guessing game, wondering constantly if he likes you or not. I was like the first slice of bread in the packet; everybody kept touching me but nobody really wanted me. You know full well that we all leave back that first slice of the bread. At times I wondered, where did I go wrong? What did I do wrong? But then, I had to ask myself, what did God do right? It was exactly at this point in my life that I decided it was time to pen my feelings, and so I started.

"How did I get here yet again? I thought that part of my life was over; so, why does it seem like déjà vu? Why am I back here struggling with these spirits when I thought they had been dealt with?" I would catch myself looking at him and wondering, "Why does he even want to hang out with me? Does he even like me? Why would he?" Here again I began to believe I wasn't good enough for him, until I came to the realization, slowly but surely, that I was good enough. (SIGHHHH) Had I reverted to my old ways again?

Here I was, 'in like' with this person not knowing how he felt, thinking I wasn't good enough to be with him. How was it possible that I was preaching down the house, going to bible school, dealing with my ministry and still these feelings wanted to resurface? My mind could not be renewed in one day as I had hoped, but it was something that had to be done daily. Someone once said, "What you have chosen to believe about yourself based upon what occurred in your past, can be more powerful to your soul than the truth and who God says you are in Him."

The last straw in our 'friendlationship' came on my birthday. Yes, I know 'friendlationship' is not a word, but that very well describes what we had. A couple weeks up until my birthday, we were doing the usual hanging out, and then out of nowhere, he reverted to his distant ways. Many times I would burst my brain trying to figure out what I had done wrong, but I couldn't find anything. I remember the day of my birthday feeling happy, but by night everything changed; my happiness turned to sadness. I would get birthday wishes and-greetings throughout the day but the one person I so wanted to hear from was him, and it never happened.

I remembered checking my phone all day and night anticipating even a message but nothing came through. Hearing a greeting from someone you care about is something a girl looks forward to, right? I recall going to my friend's house that night, and while I was walking up the driveway, he was leaving. We passed each other, I said goodnight, but there was no response from him; not even a glance my way to greet me.

I went into the house and my whole countenance changed. After silently crying to myself, I then went home and bawled my eyes out. That was the last time I was about to cry for someone who didn't even care about me. I wasn't in love, but it really hurt when it came to an end. I wasn't over him, but I had made up in my mind that I was not about to waste another tear on someone who acted like I never existed. His indecision caused me to make a decision; I had to love me more than I liked him. With him not wanting me, it paved away of the beginning of me wanting myself. We never spoke again in that manner after that; it's not like it mattered to him, anyway. He was as cool as a cucumber while I was going through the 'getting over him' process. I never received a message or call from him.

Maybe I was just a means of passing time. Sometimes opening our eyes maybe the most painful thing we have to do, but it needs to be done. My heart should not be a home for cowards and I was not about to allow it any more. Did I get over him right away? Of course not, but my feelings had to take the backseat this time and from then on. I remember hearing God as plain as day. Once again He said, "I told you countless times already; stop looking for love in all the wrong places. While you were craving his attention, I was craving yours; while you wanted him to spend time with you, I wanted you to spend more time with me; while you were panting after him, I wanted you to pant after me."

Being saved doesn't mean I won't go through anything, but it changes how I deal with it. Someone once told me, "Why worry about something you have no control over?" And that someone was him. Funny, right? So why should I have sleepless nights worrying about something I couldn't control? Do you know what happens when you place things in the seat next to you? People will assume that the seat is already taken. How could the man God had for me come into my life when I had luggage in the chair? Despite being only 'friends' my time was consumed with him because I had the illusion that one day I may have an ending with him. Baby girl, don't be blind. God gives us warning signs and shows us a way of escape but we choose to ignore. We tend to get so caught up in all the hype that we refuse to stop and pay attention to those 'red' lights that are blaring.

Through all the relationships I had encountered, I learnt to deal with them better each time. I am thankful for my struggles because without them I wouldn't have stumbled across my strength. It took some time for me to realize that had Brad and I ended up together I would have settled for less than God's best for me. Remember He said, "Nothing but the best, Princess!" It's so funny how I allowed these guys to stay in my life when I already knew the best God had for me.

I recalled dreams God had shown me of my husband and despite not being able to see his face, God would always show me his character. None of the men I had met thus far was like this man. But hey! I still ignored it. I realized the love I had to offer was not for everyone and with him giving up on me, it actually granted me the freedom to establish something real with the person who would want and love me. Just because something doesn't work out in your life, doesn't mean that you're under satanic attack. Sometimes we just put ourselves in situations. Honnney! You are not a toy to be played with and then tossed aside. Don't let yourself be caught settling for random guys who clearly don't deserve your heart. Some people, no matter what you do, will never recognize your worth and that's quite okay. You should not have to beg, force or give yourself to someone to make them see your worth.

Make sure that whoever you give access to your life will identify that you are indeed marriage material and not just someone to pass time with. Sometimes not getting what you want is a wonderful thing. And sometimes God doesn't give you what you want, not because you don't deserve it, but because you deserve so much better. What I found out through my experience with Brad is that I was trying to pick fruit when the season wasn't even ripe.

In all honesty I do not regret anything, I tend not to do regrets in life. I take full responsibility for everything that transpired because I was the predator and he was the prey. I saw him, and wanted him badly, never taking into consideration that he didn't want me. I pursued him when he was the one who should have been pursing me. It was not his fault that he wasn't interested; it was clearly my fault for I was too desperate.

Trying to get someone to like you will leave you with a broken heart.

Dear Diary,

Maybe I was someone to past time with. I never mattered, so when the clock hit, "I'm bored with her", it was over faster than it had begun. I had exhausted my heart over someone who never cared about me to begin with. I was drawn to the mystery he held, and that was what I fell for. I honestly thank him for breaking my heart the way he did, because despite the hurt and the pain, I learned to love me.

Chapter 10

Who's Sitting In the Seat Beside You?

Let's go back to a point I made in the last chapter. Do you have any idea what happens when you place your luggage in the seat beside you? People will assume that the seat is already taken. My question to you is: Are you really single? For a long time my status was single. But was I really single? No, I wasn't. One day God spoke to me and said, "How can I give you to your king when you still have those jokers around?" I was shocked because as far as I knew, I was not in a physical relationship. He further explained how I was still carrying around my exes spiritually and that they needed to go.

God cannot send your king until you've removed the jokers. You have to physically and spiritually remove the excess baggage out of your life and allow God to heal you before He can give you to the heart that's meant to love you. I mentioned earlier about soul ties and the deposit a male makes, particularly through sexual intercourse. This was what God was referring to. My soul was tied together with them in the spiritual realm. I had only had sex with two guys in my life; but, two was way too much because they had left me with STDs - 'Sexually Transmitted Demons'. My soul was still knitted together with theirs and for me to be really single, I needed deliverance.

I read somewhere that, every time we have a sexual experience, we create deep rooted, invisible bonds with the other individual. Soul ties between married couples draw them together like magnets, and it is the same way when we engage in sexual activity outside of marriage. However, those soul ties are dangerous because they are outside the covenant of marriage and must be dealt with spiritually, or we will forever be bombarded with unwholesome thoughts and feelings towards another person.

I was carrying past hurts and feelings from the previous relationships and all that baggage was making it impossible for God to place me with my king. So my question to you is, how many jokers are you walking around with? How many people have you spiritually, emotionally and mentally knitted yourself to? You need to remove from your life. I'm sorry to break it to you, but you're not single; you are still in relationship or relationships that must finally come to an end.

1 Corinthians 6:15-17 Do you not know that your bodies are members of Christ? Shall I then take the members of Christ and make them members of a harlot? Certainly not! Or do you not know that he who is joined to a harlot is one body with her? For "the two," He says, "shall become one Flesh." But he who is joined to the Lord is one spirit with Him.

Another question to you is - are you physically single? Even though your status may be single, can your king look at you and know that you are free or are there jokers still hanging around taking up residence? You may be waiting on God to bring Mr. Right for you but God is probably waiting on you to hurry up and remove those Mr. Wrongs from your life. Don't be like me and waste time bringing a joker into your kingdom and have him take up space.

Despite not being in a 'relationship' per se, I was still entertaining people who were taking up space in my life. I was the girl to hang with until the Mrs. Right was found. Are you that girl? I had to make the decision to sweep house and remove the baggage. Why keep someone around who refuses to make a commitment to you, when someone else is waiting to wife you up? As long as it seems that you're taken, even though you're not, a good man will stay away.

Some of you may have a guy in your life and you say, "Oh, we are just friends". But if you are honest with yourself, you will confess that you are keeping close because you are hoping to have a 'one day' with him. You are putting your hope in someone who may eventually leave you hopeless and broken. You need to find out from him exactly what he wants and if it isn't you, then you need to get stepping and stop clinging. You are putting your life on hold for a man who hasn't made a commitment to you. You say you are just friends but when a girl comes around you get mad. STOP LYING TO YOURSELF. Let him shape up or you need to ship out.

You need to stop messing with your own heart and get it right. Are you single ? Or do you have a 'friend' who is stopping you from meeting your king? You have to make the decision to clear your house and remove anything that does not belong. Stop trying to crown a clown; it's time to move on. A king knows you are worthy of marriage, but a clown will put you through the ringer and still never give you a ring. Stop wasting your time with a man who is barely putting any effort into you. Aren't you tired of wasting your time with those jokers? Then make room for a true king, baby girl.

Who do you have in your life that may be stopping you from receiving your blessing? Let's look at the story of Abraham. He was told by God to leave his country and his family. God had explained to him that He would bless him and make his name great. However, he was disobedient and took his nephew Lot with him. While reading on in the story we see that there was a split between Abraham and Lot's people and soon there was a separation. It was only then, after the departure of Lot that God lifted up Abraham's eyes.

Genesis 13:14-18 And the Lord said to Abram, after Lot had separated from him: "Lift your eyes now and look from the place where you are—northward, southward, eastward, and westward; for all the land which you see I give to you and your descendants forever. And I will make your descendants as the dust of the earth; so that if a man could number the dust of the earth, then your descendants also could be numbered. Arise, walk in the land through its length and its width, for I give it to you." Then Abram moved his tent, and went and dwelt by the terebinth trees of Mamre, which are in Hebron, and built an altar there to the Lord.

It is said that sometimes the best way to add to your life is to subtract from it. We have to get rid of some of those 'Lots' in our lives and make ourselves ready for the blessing God has for us. God is waiting on you to make room for Him to work with. It's time for a spring cleaning. All the clutter is keeping you from getting where you need to go; congestion stinks. We all have the natural tendency to cling to what is familiar, even it if proves detrimental to us; we witnessed this with Abraham. Don't be stubborn and try to hold onto what God wants you to leave behind. If you know you have to let go, then let go.

When God asks you to put down something, He replaces it with something better. The cleaning process may be a bit difficult and challenging, especially for hoarders, but I guarantee you it will be worth it. Not only will your kingdom be much lighter and burden free, but you will have the room for God to send your king to rule that kingdom. When Abraham removed Lot and got his life in order, God then started to move. When you get your spiritual life in order, your physical life will fall into place. Get to cleaning.

Dear Diary,

My closet is cleaned; the garbage is gone and left sitting at the heap. I will no longer entertain jokers but leave space for my king - a man who will commit and not compromise. And one day he will say, "Will you marry me?" I am single! Yessssss! I am really single!

Chapter 11

Goodbye & Hello

Matthew 6:14-15 *For if you forgive men their trespasses, your heavenly Father will also forgive you. But if you do not forgive men their trespasses, neither will your Father forgive your trespasses.*

Life becomes easier when we stop allowing people to control us. How are we allowing them to do this? It is by having unforgiveness in our hearts. It keeps you in bondage while making you immobile to the will of God. It's time to say goodbye to unforgiveness and hello to freedom. There is a story in **Matthew 18:21-35** about the unforgiving servant. This man owed his master ten thousand talents but was unable to pay. He and his family were ordered to be sold so that the debt could be settled, but after crying out to his master for mercy, he was shown compassion, released and forgiven his debt.

The servant then went out and found one of his fellow servants who owed him a hundred denarii but instead of showing compassion and mercy the same way his master had shown him, he laid hands on his fellow servant, took him by the throat, demanding that he be paid what he was owed. The man fell at his feet and begged him for forgiveness, but he refused to show such compassion and had him thrown into prison until he could pay the debt. This man wanted the forgiveness of his master but refused to show the same forgiveness. How wrong is this? Many of us do this today as well. He was forgiven much by his master, yet could not return that forgiveness to a man who owed him so little.

The Bible states that when someone hurts us, we are under an obligation to God to forgive that person. How can we expect God to forgive us when we hold grudges and resentment against others? How could I have expected God to forgive me of my fornication, wickedness and disobedience, yet blatantly refuse to forgive the people who hurt me? I wanted something that I didn't want to give in return; IMPOSSIBLE. If we receive forgiveness from God, we must give it to others. Jesus was very clear on this. Forgiveness is to set a prisoner free and that prisoner is you.

Don't continue to let yourself be held hostage. Forgiveness is a choice and not a feeling. Joseph is a phenomenal example of someone who forgave others, even though from our perspective, they did not deserve it. He was betrayed by his brothers, which led to him being kidnapped, enslaved, and imprisoned. Joseph's brothers were out to destroy him because of their hatred and jealousy towards him; nevertheless, although their intention was to kill him, he readily forgave them.

Genesis 45:14-15 Then he fell on his brother Benjamin's neck and wept, and Benjamin wept on his neck. Moreover he kissed all his brothers and wept over them, and after that his brothers talked with him.

Genesis 50:20 But as for you, you meant evil against me; but God meant it for good, in order to bring it about as it is this day, to save many people alive.

Joseph did not let the actions of his brothers turn him into a person he was not. We should never let the mistreatment of others poison our spirit. We have to forgive in order for our prayers to be answered and for God to work His perfect will. I am of the strong belief you should forgive; however, that forgiveness does not mean I have to forget. I believe in forgiving and very quickly before any resentment, revenge and bitterness festers. I will forgive, but I don't want to forget. Why? I don't want to forget the late nights I cried myself to sleep, the times he cheated, the many excuses he made, the feeling of not being good enough and the times I was completely ignored.

I remember, because it makes me stronger and helps me understand why I shouldn't answer the phone when he calls, or why I should ignore his 'I miss you' messages. I will forgive you, we will be cool and all, but me remembering allows me not to fall into that trap that he may very well want to set up again. When you forget a snake is a snake, you will definitely be bitten again. You should have the love of God in your heart to forgive that snake, but don't forget the traps he set in order to avoid falling again.

We should never let the circumstances of life make us dry. Many times we make excuses for our bitterness and unforgiveness , believing that because of our past pain we should automatically be mean. We have a right to feel anger when we've been hurt, but that doesn't give us the right to let it cripple us. We should never let our struggle become our identity. The past is the past and we have to move on. You cannot make the person that God has for you pay for what your exes did. Show them that despite the hurt and the pain they've caused, you can still love again.

Love hard like you've never been hurt before. Forgive like you've never been broken before. Relationships have their challenges without complicating them with things of the past. Love didn't hurt you; a person who didn't know how to love did. You cannot expect God to send you someone new when you still refuse to forgive the people who inflicted pain. If you cannot forgive, then you are not ready for marriage. You will be marrying an imperfect human who will also need forgiveness, so get it right from the start. Forgive the people who have done you wrong. Every woman deserves a man that will make her forget her heart was once broken, but you have to be ready to receive that love. To do that, you have to forgive the people who caused you pain. One day someone will walk into your life and make you see why it never worked out with anyone else. It's up to you to make a clear way to receive your blessing.

If you choose not to release those persons and continue to nurse the injury and harbor resentment, then you should be prepared for some major consequences. When you forgive, the problems of the past will no longer dictate your destiny. Freedom is yours if you would only decide to say goodbye to unforgiveness. In letting go of that unforgiveness, you open the door to peace, joy and happiness. When I forgave all the people in my past that hurt me severely, I felt a weight lifted. They no longer affected me negatively because I chose to forgive. It's safe to say that I even have relationships with some of these people and I am able to communicate with them better. Forgiveness is the key to unlocking many doors; no way will I allow anyone to hinder the blessings God has in store for me.

Unforgiveness means we desire to hurt the people who have wounded us. It's like the little boy who was sitting on a park bench in obvious agony. A man walking by asked him what was wrong. The boy answered, "I'm sitting on a bumble bee." "Then why don't you get up?" the man asked. The boy replied, "Because I figure that I am hurting him more than he is hurting me!" The healing process begins when we get up off the park bench. God will only heal our wounds when we stop inflicting pain on the one who hurt us. ~Kent Crockett, The 911 Handbook, Peabody~

<u>Throw off Those Clothes and Anoint Yourself</u>

You will begin to heal when you forgive and let go of the past. I thank God each day for not bringing my 'boo' aka my king before I was ready. If He had done that, I honestly believe I would have broken him. He would be dealing with a heart broken by other men. Hurt people hurt people as I previously said, but healed people also heal people. The right thing at the wrong time is still the wrong thing. All the time I thought I was ready for a relationship, but truth is, I was not. I was damaged and messed up and needed to be healed before I could even think about giving myself to someone else. A healed person has so much to give, but a damaged person does not.

Healing is not an overnight process as some may think; it is a daily cleansing of pain. We have to make the conscious decision to walk away from the darkness and into the light of that healing. There is only one person who can mend and heal a broken heart and make it better than it was before and that is God Himself. After you have removed the jokers from your life, it is time to start the healing process. The unforgiveness, pain, hurt and disappointments you have encountered need to be laid aside and you have to walk into the healing arms of Jesus. Heartbreak is something that we all will encounter at some point in our lives, but we have to know when it is time to get up, heal, and move on. Read (**2 Samuel 12:15-24**) David was in a situation where he was experiencing heartbreak and pain, nevertheless, he recovered and was even stronger because of it. He was mourning and refused to eat; he was broken and cried out to God.

David seemed so distraught, that his servants were even gravely afraid to inform him that his son had died. The Bible says, "So David arose from the ground, washed and anointed himself, and changed his clothes; and he went into the house of the Lord and worshiped. Then he went to his own house; and when he requested, they set food before him, and he ate." The child had died and he found no use in crying anymore. Your situation is dead and it is time you begin to heal and move on.

While you were in the situation you may have fasted and prayed to God to give you answers in hope that everything may turn out the way you wanted, but it didn't. So what are you to do now? Does it make sense to continue to mourn after the dead? God has already told you that man is not for you, but you continue to hold on and wallow in self-pity continually exhausting your heart. Girl, you need to move on! Let the dead be! The time of mourning and weeping is no more but a time of healing is upon you. Get up and wash yourself, change your clothes and anoint your head. God has something new for you but you have to let go of the old and walk into your healing.

You cannot start the next chapter of your life if you keep trying to stay in the previous one. Weeping may endure for a night, but joy comes in the morning. After the death of his son, Bathsheba gave birth to Solomon and God wants to also do a new thing for you. David let go of the dead and something new was birthed. What are you going to do? Sometimes we have to stop acting so wounded, lift our heads up and wipe those tears. Stuff may affect us but we should not let it break us. Situations will make us bend, but we should never let them break us. When everything may seem as if it's falling apart, it may be very well falling into place.

Dear Diary,

And I thought I wouldn't make it after the heartbreak, wondering how life would be without them. "It just wouldn't be the same, I would never be happy again," I lamented. I thought for a while that my heart had stopped beating. But look at me now, living and feeling happy; look at my heart now, beating stronger than ever. Something bad happened and I had two choices: to let it strengthen me or destroy me. I opted for the first. My old clothes I have torn; my head I have anointed and now I am free.

Chapter 12

Purity Over Lust

1 Thessalonians 4:3-5 For this is the will of God, your sanctification: that you should abstain from sexual immorality; that each of you should know how to possess his own vessel in sanctification and honor, not in passion of lust, like the Gentiles who do not know God.

Purity seems to be considered old fashion and irrelevant in the world we live in today. How do I stay pure? By trusting God and not myself; don't be fooled; "This flesh ain't loyal". It will indeed fail you if you place your trust in it; not trusting you is the best thing for you. Intimacy is not sex; you can keep your legs closed and still be intimate. Intimacy is closeness, and that, sweetheart, is something you can have without sex. Let that man touch your mind and your spirit without touching your body illegally. A real man can and will love you without the benefits of sex.

Celibacy isn't easy, so whoever said it was, was definitely lying. But sleeping with a man who doesn't desire your heart, and breaking your vow with God is much worse. Thus, I do not want or ask for easy, because me being pure before God is an honor. Purity goes beyond having sexual intercourse. Often times we believe that staying pure means not having penetrative sex, but any form of sex, outside of marriage is detestable to God. It even goes beyond that. We have to stay pure in the way we dress and speak as well.

I made the promise, as I had said years before, that the next time I had sex, it would be with my husband, but I still found myself doing things that were definitely not pure. I remember using my mouth to speak unholy things, thinking it didn't matter but it actually did. I dressed sexy and in very revealing clothing, cleavage showing and short skirts, and I never thought anything of it. The fewer clothes the more likes. But you are just selling yourself like a piece of meat. What was the harm in getting a little attention, right?

CAUTION! I was trying to gain illegitimate attention and so I attracted horn dogs. I was making guys lust after me and that was very intentional and wrong. No wonder I kept getting the wrong type of guy. GO FIGURE! The type of bait you throw out will determine the type of fish you catch. Men are very visual, so you need to be weary of the signals you are giving them. You walk around saying how pure you are with your mouth but prance around in front of guys looking like fornication itself. STOP IT!

Someone said, "If your goal is to dress sexy, more than likely you will attract guys whose goal is to have sex." I was so empty inside that I resorted to gaining attention the wrong way and that was with my body. I then attracted guys who were led by their penis instead of a godly man who is led by the Spirit. In her book, More Than a Hero: Muhammad Ali's Life Lessons Through His Daughter's Eyes, Hana Ali shares an interesting encounter she had with her dad after she came to his house in quite some revealing clothing. She recalled him saying:

"Everything that God made valuable in the world is covered and hard to get to. Where do you find diamonds? Deep down in the ground, covered and protected. Where do you find pearls? Deep down at the bottom of the ocean, covered up and protected in a beautiful shell. Where do you find gold? Way down in the mine, covered over with layers and layers of rock. You've got to work hard to get to them. Your body is sacred. You're far more precious than diamonds and pearls, and you should be covered too."

If we want to be respected as women of virtue then we must present our physical bodies in a way that a man of God can take notice. Don't say you want your king yet you act like Jezebel. When you remove sex and sexual behavior, you remove the men who are only pursuing you for sex. We have to take a stand and cover our bodies and expose our minds. Sex is a gift worth giving and you will not only be honoring God with your purity but your future husband as well.

I love the fact that my husband will know that even though I was tempted and tried, I fought through, hence saving myself for him. My body is a gift for my husband to unwrap. How blessed is he! (HAHA) You had better believe it. Every decision you make now will affect the purity of your marriage, so be careful. I decided to make a vow of purity before God and

I sealed the deal with a purity ring. Choosing to wear a ring should be your choice and it is not a stipulation. Nevertheless, I wear it boastfully because it's an outward symbol of the inward commitment I've made to God and my future husband.

That day was awesome to me and I would forever remember that little commitment service I held myself, for myself, in the confinements of my bedroom. I got the olive oil and anointed my body before God, making a vow to be always pure in every way possible. It was so touching that I cried, with the snot and all (Lol). I broke down before my Daddy and told Him everything I may have struggled with, and asked Him to be my strength in my times of temptation ahead. I don't play the innocent game, God already knows me inside and out.

My love language is physical touch, so I definitely needed to make sure I asked for a double portion of strength and anointing until my hubby comes along and we start courting. I may not have had sex with some of the men I had dated or had been "friends" with, but the fondling, grabbing, kissing and touching stirred up my appetite, and I had a need for more. In the process of courting, you should know what turns you on and avoid it at all costs. Don't be afraid to run, girl. "Run, Forest, runnnnnnn!!!"

There is no doubt that at some point you will be tempted. Just because you are a Christian doesn't mean you won't be sexually tempted. Being tempted is not a sin. Jesus was tempted as well. It is when you give into the temptation that the real problems begin. I chose to use the words "I have decided" for my ring. I have decided to remain abstinent, to stay pure in my speech, dress and conduct, to set boundaries at all times, to honor God and my husband with my body. The scripture that I fell in love with and made an inscription on my ring was:

*2 **Chronicles** 15:7 But you, be strong and do not let your hands be weak, for your work shall be rewarded.*

I shall be rewarded; YES, indeed. I also made the decision not to kiss before my wedding day. Choosing not to kiss before marriage is not a law of any sorts. If you decide to kiss before your wedding, you will not go to hell. So please never tell anyone I said not kissing before marriage is obligatory. Kissing leads to other things and other things lead to vow breaking and that is not a risk I am willing to take. To me, it's a demonstration of virtue and shows a great amount of discipline and self-control. Some people do not believe in my decision but hey, it's my decision.

Every relationship will not have the same boundaries that I have chosen, so if you choose to kiss before marriage please note that it doesn't make you a bad person. As for me, I just made the decision not to. Will it be hard? YES, it will be. Did I make the decision on my own without even having a spouse as yet? YES. It is important that you set your boundaries beforehand. Before you have a discussion with your partner about boundaries, you first need to clearly define your own boundaries. You have to decide where your line is drawn before you find yourself in a compromising situation.

The man of integrity God has for you will respect and honor you and your vows. I will never apologize for my standards because the man who wants to be in my life will rise up to meet them. A man afraid of breaking God's heart will make my purity a priority and will run the race with me. Setting boundaries is a must for us to remain pure. If you have no boundaries, then a man has nothing to stop him from doing whatever he wants with you.

Boundaries are something I had never done before in a thorough sense. When talking to someone I would let it be known very well that I would not be having sex before marriage. Automatically I believed that they knew this statement meant sex and anything dealing with it and around those lines; but we cannot and should not assume that they know. We have to be straight, clear and concise with our boundaries and let the guy know what we expect from him. My friend would chime in at this point and say, she feels for my future husband. I mean, come on now, my rules are not so tough. Because of bad experiences in the past and the many hiccups, I am very precise in what I want and what I expect of the man who will go to my Daddy for my hand in marriage.

I have no time to play games and waste time. I have no intention of dating random guys. #NORANDOMZ is my policy. I have learnt a lot because I've been through a lot. And because of it all, I've become wiser. I know now what I want and what I will not accept and that should go for you as well. Additionally, we have to be very careful with the books we read and the movies we watch. We live in a lustful world and these images can play a lot with our minds, creating problems. If you submit your mind to these things that undermine your values, you are heading for trouble.

Baby girl you cannot say you are against adultery but yet sit down to watch a series which endorses adultery week after week. What are you feeding your spirit? Where has your values gone? Girl, you need to quit watching that filth while you are ahead. It's very important for us to control our thoughts and not allow our thoughts to control us. "Be careful little eyes what you see". Jesus Himself said it.

Matthew 6:22-23 The lamp of the body is the eye. If therefore your eye is good, your whole body will be full of light. But if your eye is bad, your whole body will be full of darkness. If therefore the light that is in you is darkness, how great is that darkness!

You cannot expect to watch a movie with extreme sexual content and come out untouched spiritually. If you feed the flesh then you begin to stir up yourself in more ways than one. You may think that it's not a big deal until you start to realize sometime after that your lust issues are beginning to creep back in. By feeding your spirit garbage, you are giving the enemy legal grounds to tamper with you.

Masturbation is also another impure act that is WRONG. I have heard many people say, "It's not in the Bible so that means it's quite okay. "WRONG! Administering immediate sexual gratification to yourself is okay? If that is the way you think, then you need to align yourself to the will of God. Masturbation is done in isolation and is accompanied with lust. Why would you hide something if it's okay? Why should you feel ashamed if it's okay? Never let anyone tell you that since you are not having sex, masturbation is a harmless way to relieve sexual tension and stress. Yes! I've also heard this before as well.

Whenever you're not sure about something and you stand in the grey area, always consult God, after all, He is the truth. Many people secretly struggle with masturbation because they are ashamed and afraid to speak out and ask for help. I understand this fully well, I may not have been addicted to masturbation, but I've done it, I had my share of lusting. Do not isolate yourself and believe that you are alone in the matter. If you're struggling with the issue of masturbation, get it dealt with quickly.

Woman of worth, you have no time for games, you have to make up in your mind that "no ring means NO thing; no wedding means NO bedding". Don't let anyone fondle you just because you believe you are in love; never compromise your morals and values for anyone. Don't believe that you have to settle for a man who wants to feel all over you, pressure you into doing something outside the will of God. A true man of God will fight alongside you to help you stay pure. Don't worry about that man finding you or loving you without giving him your body. He will recognize the Spirit of God in you and not recognize you by the shape and feel of your body.

No one should have to force you to live pure but it should be a desire you have. If you truly love God, then you will have that desire to live pure. The world says you must test the car before you buy it, but God says "I know what kind of car you like so trust Me." A real man will lead a woman closer to Christ and not his bedroom. A man is supposed to be searching for his rib and not breasts and thighs. As Christians we should want to abstain from sex until marriage because we love God and because that is what He has commanded. It will be a challenge; temptations will come, but it will be worth it. Kris Vallotton said, "Love is a sacrifice and love isn't love until it has cost you something." It cost God His Son on the cross for you, so why is it that you cannot abstain from a little pleasure for however long?

"Anyone can give away something expensive, but only those who understand sacrifice can give away something valuable."
~ Kris Vallotton

Romans 6:12-13 *Do not let sin reign in your mortal body, that you should obey it in its lusts. And do not present your members as instruments of unrighteousness to sin, but present yourselves to God as being alive from the dead, and your members as instruments of righteousness to God.*

Dear Diary,

I smile when people ask, "How can you not have sex? Isn't it hard? Has it really been that long and don't you want to?" And the questions go on and on. To me, it's very simple. My sacrifice is nothing compared to the one Jesus made for me. Sex does not control me. I will constantly feed my spirit and starve my flesh. Nothing I do is of my strength but of His. As for me and my body we will honor and serve the Lord.

Chapter 13

UGLY - U Gotta Love You

Psalm 139:14 *I will praise You, for I am fearfully and wonderfully made; Marvelous are Your works, And that my soul knows very well.*

You are precious to God but how precious are you to yourself? I would lie in my bed at night and couldn't sleep because I was fighting myself; a whole world war was going on in my head. When everything went quiet, I was screaming inside. I was rejected all my life from the time I came out the womb and I never thought I was good enough for anything or anyone. Have you ever fought demons all your life? If you know what I'm talking about then you would understand how I felt.

No matter how much people would tell me how beautiful I was, talented, etc., I would never see it. I never loved myself so how could I expect someone else to love me? I hated mirrors, constantly being my own worst critic. In my opinion, nearly everything about me needed fixing, but what really needed fixing was my soul; it needed surgery, it needed to be adjusted to the Word of God. For many years I kept adding layers of masks to hide how I really felt. I was like a magician, hiding the hurt and pain from the people around me with a very big fake smile. I tried my best to fix everything on the outside that I didn't like. Something was always too big or too small. But as I said, the inside needed fixing. My soul needed to be changed drastically.

We can use Band-Aids for outside wounds but when it comes to the pain on the inside, only Jesus Himself and His blood can heal those. It is very important to know whose you are and who you are in Christ, or the enemy will fill your head with lies about who he wants you to believe you are. My soul was in agony from the time I knew myself and no matter how much I tried, I just couldn't see what people saw.

So many Christian women walk around without identity and this is one of the reasons why they settle for less; they do not believe they deserve better. When you have no identity you are lost. The devil was infiltrating my mind. Stronghold thinking can affect those who deeply love the Lord, so don't get it twisted. I loved my Daddy but I had to renew my mind. New life comes from a new mindset. It is said that if you can kill it in your head, you can kill it in your life, and I needed to kill it in my head. I had to get into the routine of renewing my mind daily. It was only obvious that if Satan had spent so many years filling my head with lies, it would take time to fill it with truth. It did not happen overnight, but it eventually happened.

"She looked in the mirror and realized how special she was, the value that was upon her. She finally saw the beauty she couldn't see before. Only then did she realize she didn't have to settle for second best. She understood that she was worth so much more.

Despite her flaws, she now knew that she was never to be placed
on sale. When she understood how much she was worth, she
stopped giving those discounts. Most importantly, she knew what
God thought of her, in spite of her past and the wrongs that she
had done, He saw a Queen, royalty at its best. No more would she
sell herself for cheap hire." –Shaniqua L. Howell

When I learnt to accept and love myself, only then was I aware of what I deserved. All the things I thought I wasn't good enough to do, I then started to accomplish, including writing this book. What would you do if you believed that you were good enough? A lot of the time, we really don't know what we are entitled to. You have to stop letting the enemy run your life and take back control. Even if someone rejects you, that's ok boo, don't worry about it, it doesn't decrease your value, you are still valuable. My mentality became very simple after I started to truly love me.

It took me many years, a lot of pain and struggles for me to learn how to love myself. So it's either you like me or you don't, I have neither time nor energy to waste trying to convince someone that I am worth it. I already know what I bring to the table, so if you fail to see my worth, then it's your loss. I no longer have to degrade and put myself down and walk around with my head lowered. The royalty that I possess as a child of the King will ooze through my being and attract a man of God, and not an imp of Satan. I kept attracting the type of men I did because I never believed I deserved better. When you reach that realization, everything will begin to change for you.

I am not worthless because God does not make worthless things. I am not who the devil says I am, but I am who God says I am, a daughter of the King. I am a joint heir with Christ, seated in heavenly places. I am not a hired servant but a Son. My worth is no longer determined by man but by God. When you know your worth, no one can make you feel worthless. Kudos to the people in my past who put me down and made me feel as if I didn't matter; because of it all, I am a stronger and a better me. I am unique, baby, there's no other like me. I am not conceited, I am confident; I just happen to know who I am and whose I am. It's not vanity but me understanding my identity.

To the girl who may be reading this book, with those thoughts of-unworthiness and low self-worth, self- confidence is your best outfit, so wear it. My prayer for you is that you quickly recognize who you are and whose you are. Your worth is far above rubies and gold. Stop settling for less than the best. Rest and abide in what God says and block out the lies of man and the devil. Bind your mind to the mind of Christ; moreover, bind your will to the will of Christ. Stop being your own worst critic sis and become your own raving fan. In order for someone else to love you, you have to first love yourself.

Luke 10:27 So he answered and said, You shall love the Lord your God with all your heart, with all your soul, with all your strength, and with all mind, and 'your neighbor as yourself.'

We cannot love others if we don't love ourselves first. If you treat yourself like the queen that you are, then you will attract a king. Stop hating yourself for everything that you aren't and start loving yourself for everything that you are. It's time to throw away those preconceived ideas you hold so dear in your head, and listen to what God has to say about you. You are royalty.

Song of Solomon 4:7 *You are all fair, my love, and there is no spot in you.*

Guard your heart!

Proverbs 4:23 Keep your heart with all diligence, for out of it spring the issues of life.

God won't trust anyone with your heart, so why should you? Don't be deceived by those butterflies in your stomach. Be very careful about who you are giving your heart to. It's very easy to say hello but much harder to say goodbye. Never let a random guy poison your heart for the one that it is meant for. Build a fence around that heart, not a wall. Build a fence and make sure you build it with a gate. You control the lock. The Holy Spirit will show you who to open that gate to.

Guard your heart but also discern when to take the risk. We cannot leave our hearts out in the open and expect them not to be trampled on. Some of us blame God for all our pain and heartache but most of our pain comes from our disobedience. We willingly give away our hearts to clowns and expect them not to joke around with it. The devil doesn't come with a cape and some horns; he comes as everything you wish for, because he too knows what you like, your preferences and your weakness. He will send someone your way; therefore, we have to be guarded. We have to be extremely careful about the people we let into our lives. It's very easy to let someone into your heart but hard to get them out.

Dear Diary,

A queen wearing her crown will hold her head up high; she does not have an identity crisis for she knows her worth and value. She is a queen. She knows her virtue and that she is to be highly praised. The Proverbs 31 woman -that's who she is. She has been given honor and dignity. She smiles brightly because she knows to whom she belongs. She is the daughter of the King, the Most High God. I am made in the image of God and refuse to look at the images in a magazine to define who I am or should be. I am a woman of Virtue, Integrity, Purpose and Strength; I shall continue to guard and protect my heart. No longer a home for the men of the devil, I will leave it reserved for a man of God. I am soooooo worth it.

Chapter 14

Season of Singleness

It's Ok To Be Single

There is a stigma set to the word 'single', leaving most Christian women afraid of being single, which causes them to miss the benefits of this season of their lives. If you have a desire for marriage then trust God and wait on Him; He hasn't forgotten you. Being single gives you unlimited time with Christ whilst the married person has to worry about the house, bills, children, and her husband. The woman in her season of singleness gets to focus her attention solely on Christ.

1 Corinthians 7:32-33 But I want you to be without care. He who is unmarried cares for the things of the Lord, how he may please the Lord. But he who is married cares about the things of the world, how he may please his wife.

Singleness is not a disease but rather a season in your life that you should cherish and embrace. It should be a state to pursue and not to be avoided. We can become distracted thirsting after marriage, making it an idol that we miss so much in our time of singleness. There is much that can be gained in your waiting.

Isaiah 40:31 But those who wait on the Lord shall renew their strength; they shall mount up with wings like eagles, they shall run and not be weary, they shall walk and not faint.

Despite what some may believe, the world did not begin with a marriage, it began with a single man - Adam. In his season of singleness, Adam was being prepared to receive Eve. After all the work was completed, God then told Adam it was not good for him to be alone. God's focus with you is not marriage first, it's your singleness. He is interested in developing you. Marriage is the second stage and not the first one. Chill, baby girl! I was one out of many who hated my singleness in the beginning. I would groan regularly and asked God to hurry up and send me my husband. Little did I know that God was working on me.

I was caught up with wanting a companion that I did not realize the importance of this alone time with just me and my Daddy. He wanted to iron out some wrinkles He saw in me; He wanted to spend more time with me; He wanted me to do all I could do and wanted to do before I was married. He was building my character and molding me into the proper wife that my husband needed. I was single because my future husband deserved a woman who was better than I was at that time. He deserved the best version of me and not the broken version. God was giving me His best so He had to make sure I was His best for my Boo. My time of singleness was a process of pruning and grooming. Stress and loneliness will make you believe that everything has to happen right now, but that's a big old lie.

Marriage is not the solution to any unmet needs we may have. I guarantee that if you're unhappy single, you will be unhappy married. Your life will not begin on your wedding day. Get it right, baby girl. When married, you may never again know a time like the one you're in right now. You now have a period of complete devotion to Christ without the worries of a family. To everything there is a time and a season. We have to stop being covetous of marriage and enjoy the time God has blessed us with.

Don't rush the seasons, thank God for the winter also. You may think the season of winter is harsh and not needed, but believe me when I say that it is. Winter is a time of hibernation and preparation. It is a time for us to think and get ourselves in order for the spring, which is the season of planting. When the summer comes ringing in, you will reap what you have sown. You will fully enjoy the labor of the winter and the spring season. Stop trying to push God's hand. Wait for God's man in God's perfect timing.

I remember crying out to God and asking Him if He didn't care; I wanted to know if He had forgotten about me and what was taking so long? Have you ever felt like this? Of course you have! (That-was-a-rhetorical-question). I remember the times I shouted and screamed like a toddler throwing a tantrum. I had a desire for a husband and some kids, but God, was apparently taking fairly long. What was He waiting for? I had committed myself to living pure for years and being right before Him. Then out of the blue, I would see someone getting married and my impatience grew thinner. "Seriously, God?" I would say, "How is it that I'm doing everything right and nothing is happening, but for other people, it is?"

We have to rejoice with others when they receive their blessing knowing that our time will come; there's no need for jealousy. At times I felt hopeless, as if He'd forgotten all the promises He made. Did He not care about my feelings? Did He not realize that time was running out?" I was getting older every year, and it seemed as if everyone was in a relationship or getting married - except me! "Godddddddddddd!!!!" I screamed louder. "I know for sure you really don't care about my feelings and what I want!" I bellowed. Yes, He cared. It was because He cared so much that He had kept me in this season for as long as He did. He was saving me from all the hurt and the pain and sending me through the refiner's fire.

Our biological clocks should never override the Holy Spirit. No matter how long you may think you are in the season of singleness, you have to trust that God knows what He is doing. I was not ready at the time to court or even think about being in a relationship. I needed to go through a process of healing before anyone could come into my life, but I refused to see it at the time. Let me take a look at the story of the prodigal son again, but from a different angle. The son was an heir who was entitled to an inheritance and benefits. There was nothing at all wrong with the son asking his father for his portion. The problem came when the son asked for his portion at the wrong time. How many times do we do this? Nothing is wrong with us asking God for a husband and some kids if we want.

We have to understand that Daddy does not have an issue with giving us our portion. He loves to give His children gifts, but God's timing is God's timing and we have to be very aware of that. When we try to gain things outside the timing and order of God, we then bring unwanted issues upon ourselves. Because of his impatience, the son took his inheritance at the wrong time, and this caused him to have to travel a rocky road. Does this sound familiar?

Notwithstanding your feelings of weariness, believe that God will fulfill His promise. Yes, you will have those impromptu moments of feeling lonely, but remember that God is not a man that will lie, and if He says He has that man for you, then rest assured that you will be united with him when the time is right. In the meantime, enjoy your life. Go out and date yourself. Be happy with you.

Am I satisfied?

I've come to realize that when a single person declares he/she is satisfied it raises issues and questions. Why can't a single person be satisfied? Maybe it's the misconception that you cannot be happy as a single. When I say I am satisfied, please don't take it as I never want a relationship. However, despite wanting to be in a relationship someday, I am very contented with what I have now and where I am at in this moment - totally satisfied with Christ and choosing to wait on Him. In the book of Philippians, Paul said that he learned how to be content, regardless of the state he was in; we too must adopt this attitude.

Philippians 4:11 Not that I speak in regard to need, for I have learned in whatever state I am, to be content.

It means that I no longer let my desire for a husband supersede my relationship with Christ. We can get so caught up in seeking a spouse, that we forget our first love. JESUS. In our singleness we should allow ourselves to be contented. Being lonely while being single can cause you to make bad decisions and do things that you never thought of doing. Have you ever observed how many single women have settled for less than they deserve because they were not contented and became desperate for a relationship? Society, and sad to say, sometimes the church, make us believe that if we are single, we are half a person.

As someone once said, "The word 'SINGLE' should mean more to you than 'Not Married'." I've learnt to stop looking at what I don't have and look at what I do possess. When we worry too much about what's ahead we tend to look pass the blessings we have now. Instead of sitting and grumbling about how your life sucks because you don't have a spouse, get a new perspective on things. I'm sorry but as for me, not having the responsibilities of a husband and a couple of kids at this moment is the most amazing thing. I get to do anything I want and go wherever I want. All that time you spend moaning, you can be doing so much. Don't wait until you have a family to then say, 'I should have done this before.' Stop waiting on a man and start living, there is so much God has for you to do as a single.

Who has God called you to be? What is your purpose?- Don't even think about being in a relationship until you can be happy with Christ alone. Putting everything in your life on hold until you find that person is another myth that is nothing but utter nonsense and will make you miserable. Learn to live life regardless of if you are IN or OUT of a relationship and always know that the only one who can truly satisfy the human heart is the One who made it.

Where does your focus lie?

Genesis 2:18 And the Lord God said, "It is not good that man should be alone; I will make him a helper comparable to him.

In your state of singleness, your focus should never be fixed on finding a partner. God is the one who realized Adam was alone. Adam did not go out searching for a mate. He was so busy in communion with God and the work that He had set him out to do, that he did not even notice that he was alone.

We see in scripture that God then decided to make a helper, and not just any helper, but one comparable to him. Quite often, we have this process in reverse. Our focus is not on union with God and fulfilling purpose and what He has laid out for us to do, rather it is on searching for a spouse.

My desire for marriage superseded my desire for God. I was so caught up with wanting a husband that it consumed my thoughts every day. We have to understand that God knows what we need more than we do. When you spend your time in His presence, and give Him your full attention and do the work He has called you to do, just when you least expect it, your king will show up. God promises you the desires of your heart but only when you delight in Him first. Ruth was a woman on a mission. Her focus was not on finding a husband but rather providing for her and Naomi. She had a task at hand and she was eager to fulfill it. Even though she was not searching for a husband, God was behind the scenes working things out in her favor to meet her kinsman redeemer, Boaz. Ruth had no time to sit and wonder about a husband. I love the fact that Boaz had taken an interest in her and she hadn't even noticed.

Even though he had asked her to stay close to him and not glean anywhere else, he also told her, "Let your eyes be on the field which they reap and go after them." It was only after the harvest was over that Naomi told Ruth to go to Boaz. Just like Ruth, your focus should be fixed on God and not a man. When the task has been fulfilled, Jesus will lift your head up and you will meet your king. What do you want your husband to see when he finds you? Dear woman of God, when the time is right and your season of singleness is over, God will send that husband of yours. My question is, will your husband find you working or will he find you moaning and complaining about being lonely?

Proverbs 18:22 *He who finds a wife finds a good thing, and obtains favor from the Lord.*

The Bible never said she who finds a husband. Maybe you keep running into trouble because you keep searching, when you are the one who ought to be found. You shouldn't have to put yourself out there in order to be found. You, my dear child, do not determine when the time is right; God does. What you determine is your attitude and patience during your season of waiting. Your focus should not be on anything else but solely on Christ. Dance with God and He will let the right man cut in. Be so focused on Jesus that a man has to run in order to keep up with you to say 'hi'. When that time is right, suddenly you'll see that everything will fall into place.

God knows it is not fit for you to be alone. He has someone out there who is comparable to you; therefore, in the meantime, you need to place your focus on Him and stop wallowing in self-pity. No room for pity parties! After so many failed relationships, it's time to give up and realize that you are not good at matchmaking. God is the true matchmaker. He will give you the desires of your heart but you have to abide in His presence. Stop looking for a man and meet yourself. When you are whole, you will be a blessing to your husband and not a burden. I once saw this somewhere and it stuck with me, "Marriage is not for you if you are starving for something. If you are constantly seeking marriage then you are probably not ready to be married. You will be ready in the moment when you least have need for it."

"For whatever period of time I am single, by God's grace I will be totally His in body, soul, and spirit. I will claim no time, aspirations or interests of my own and will seek only to please Him. And as a single woman, I will pursue those same qualities that God values in a wife and mother - a gentle, quiet, serving, submissive, trusting spirit. If God's plan for me is to become a wife/husband, then I will wait patiently, without fretting, until God reveals the husband/wife of His choice. In the meantime, however, marriage cannot be my pursuit. I must pursue Him." (Ps. 62:5). —Nancy Leigh DeMoss

Dear Diary,

I am fully enjoying this period of singleness. I take joy in knowing that God is making me whole for the man who will become my husband. People say that they are awaiting their other half. As for me, I am becoming a whole person while waiting on a whole person. As Michelle Mckinney Hammond once said, "God will not give me anything that is half baked." My attention is fixed on HIM and not on finding him. When the fullness of time is at hand, he will find me.

Chapter 15

Dear Queen

Your Latter Shall Be Greater

Job 8:7 Though your beginning was small, yet your latter end would increase abundantly.

The Bible tells the story of a prosperous man called Job, who lost his wealth, health, family and his standing in the community. This was a man who went through a time of pressure, stress and squeezing. His life so reminds me of the process of the olive. He was shaken, beaten and pressed. The enemy took away everything he had in hopes that he would curse God. In spite of his misfortune, he held on to God. His words were, "Though he slay me, yet will I trust in Him." In the end, Job was blessed tremendously by God. He received more than he had before his tribulations.

Job 42:12 Now the Lord blessed the latter days of Job more than his beginning; for he had fourteen thousand sheep, six thousand camels, one thousand yoke of oxen, and one thousand female donkeys.

His ending was greater than the beginning because he did not turn away from God when things were difficult. In order for your oil to run, sometimes God has to take you through the process of the olive. Your destiny is far greater than your past. It doesn't matter what you have been through because God is about to do a new thing for you. He saw every bruise, every pain and every tear you've cried and now, you will be blessed more than you can imagine, despite all that you have done and all that you have been through.

You need to confidently tell people to get ready. When God begins to release the blessings He has in store, it will be a domino effect. People won't understand the favor that will be upon you, but you would have known the cost of the oil. A new season is ahead; your best is yet to come, baby girl; just wait on it. God has been preparing you for something greater all the while. No longer will you be the caterpillar; it's time for the butterfly to spread her wings. You are destined for greatness. Get ready, it's going to happen, just wait and see, keep believing, keep trusting. He who began a good work will bring it to completion.

"An olive has to go through three stages, for its oil to run: It has to go through the shaking, the beating, and the pressing. And just like the olive, some of you may have felt like you go through the shaking, the beating and the pressing. You went through all of that for your oil to flow. Now, your greater is coming."
~ Jekalyn Carr ~

Why Should I Wait?

When I look around I see many unhappy relationships due to rushing and not waiting on God. Just because everybody is doing something, doesn't mean you have to because you feel left out. You should never awaken love until it desires. **(Song of Solomon 8:4)** Not waiting on God is the reason so many women pass themselves around in church. Yes, I said it, now sue me. So desperately wanting a relationship, you keep dating guy after guy within your assembly until there aren't any left. Girl, I don't know who you are but you need to stop.

You are not a ball to be tossed back and forth. You do not have to go through a series of men in order to find Mr. Right for you. God has you covered. Do not go picking when the fruit isn't ripe. God has a gentleman especially tailor-made for you. The best place for a relationship to start is in the hands of God, but you have to wait and allow Him to do His job. You are not an option but a priority. God will not just hand you to anyone and consequently, you have to wait for nothing but the best.

Yes, at times you will grow impatient but you have to remember that He knows best; you may even struggle with the waiting despite knowing that good things are ahead. Have you ever looked back and said, "Well thank you Jesus I dodged that bullet?" How many times do you want to continue saying this? Isn't it wise then to wait? God will reveal the right person under the right circumstances. God always has a purpose for His delays, trust in His process. If He is making you wait, you're in good 'company. One day you will wake up next to your husband and say, "You were definitely worth it". Let God pick your mate, it will be worth the wait.

Blessed is she who believes!

Luke 1:45 Blessed is she who believed, for there will be a fulfillment of those things which were told her from the Lord.

How can there be hope after all those hiccups? The idea of loving someone and being loved in return is much greater than the hurt I have experienced in my past. I will never allow my heart to become icy and bitter due to mistakes I have made. Yes, I said the mistakes I made because I have to take responsibility for my actions and not blame the enemy for the choices I have made. I have been with guys who have left me high and dry, ones that I won't mention maybe because they aren't worth mentioning. Hahaha! The ones who told me how much I meant to them but then I found out were expecting a baby, the ones who declared their love but then found out they were in relationships on the verge on getting married. So to the ones that I wrote about, know that you are here because you have made an impact on my life.

I have learnt many lessons in life, especially what I want and what I don't want in a relationship. I truly believe someone is out there for me. Why? Because I believe in the promises of God. I had these preconceived ideas of what I thought I wanted but God showed me exactly what I needed God has a very funny sense of humor and He showed it off to me. Sometimes the person you want the most is the person you're best without. I thought I knew what was best for me until God shattered my dreams and turned them upside down and inside out - literally. Everything I said I didn't want in my husband are the things God decided I needed.

That day He spoke to me through His prophet and told me about my Mr. Right for me. I couldn't help but cry and laugh to myself. Of course I won't be able to share with you everything God said, for my own reasons (smile). Maybe by the time you are reading this, I will be in the process of either, meeting my Boo, getting to know him or planning my wedding. Only time will tell. Maybe I will write a book about our meeting and courting process. (HAHA)

I love the person I've become because I fought to become her. Whenever you see me and you see that big smile on my face and me being silly, it's because I've been through it all. Half of the things I wasn't able to record in this book; maybe another time, maybe another book. I don't take my ability to laugh without a mask lightly. I have spent years in bondage and being free is a breath of fresh air. I was stalked by demons but I was also guarded by angels.

To the woman of virtue reading this book, I know you have kissed a lot of frogs in the process of searching for your king. That's the problem right there; you need to stop searching. You don't have to worry about that man finding you, if you go to the Sahara Desert, when God's timing is right He will send that man on a camel to find you. Do you want to wait on God's best or will you continue to pick illegally?

You cannot expect God to bless any mess you put yourself in, so do the best thing and wait on Him. You are a good woman and you deserve a good man- a man who will love you as Christ loves the church, one who will cherish you and never make you question your worth. You have to believe and trust in God and His promise. In the meantime, never, ever compromise. When you compromise, you will complicate the promise God has for you. While you wait on your God given promise, pursue God the way you would want that man to pursue you.

Do I regret anything in my past? No. Although I dislike my past I am not ashamed of it. It is said that sometimes we learn more from tragic endings than from happy ones. Each experience has made me wiser; I am extremely proud of my heart. It's been stepped on many times yet it still has the ability to beat harder each time. A lot of things went wrong but it all ended up right. Some beautiful things have come forth from my pain; faith got me through it all. That sad, broken, depressed, stressed, tormented girl is now a mighty woman of God. She walks with her head held high, on a mission to fulfill the purpose that is upon her life. She stands firm in the promises of her Savior and until her king shows up, she is busy with the work of the Kingdom.

Lamentations 3:25 *The Lord is good to those who wait for Him, to the soul who seeks Him.*

Proverbs 3:5-6 *Trust in the Lord with all your heart, and lean not on your own understanding; In all your ways acknowledge Him, And He shall direct your paths.*

Demon: I thought I had her; I almost had her, I will sit and wait for an opportune time, I will never give up.

My Angel: Those who were with you are more than those who were against you.

God: Because you have made the Lord, your dwelling place, no evil shall befall you. What was intended to harm you, I turned it around for good to accomplish what is now being done, the saving of many lives.

Dear Diary,

I am like a tree, the enemy may try to cut me down, but I will always spring forth. My leaves may fall, my branches may sway, but I will always rise again Why? Because I am rooted in Christ. The storms of life may shake me, but they will never break me. Look at how God has made beauty from ashes. I not only survived it but I also grew from it.

To the woman who may be reading this and have not yet accepted Jesus Christ. I implore you to make a decision today. Now is the accepted time. There is a story in the Bible about a Samaritan woman with whom Jesus had an encounter. You can find this in **John Chapter 4:1-26.** This woman previously had five husbands and the one she currently had was not her own. Maybe, like me, she was looking for love in all the wrong places. Maybe she was looking for a sense of belonging but could not find it.

I may wonder and speculate on the state of this woman, but one thing I know for sure is that she was spiritually dead. She needed a man, but that man was JESUS. On having that experience with Christ, this woman was forever changed. Baby girl, I don't care how much education you have, how much money you possess and what connections you have. If you don't have Jesus, You have NOTHING. Stop delaying your salvation, because you want to play hooky with that man. Is he worth your eternity? I know a Man who will never break your heart like the others did.

I know a Man who loves you with an unconditional love like no other could. When others said you weren't worth it, He got on a cross and allowed Himself to be crucified to prove to you how much you mean to Him. He wants to shower you with love and give you a peace like never before. Jesus wants to restore you back to Him, but the choice is yours. What will you do? What is standing in your way of eternal life with Christ? I know you are ready to take this awesome step to salvation, just repeat the prayer and accept Christ into your heart today.

Dear God, I acknowledge *that I am a sinner and I ask for your forgiveness. I believe that there is only one way to heaven and that is through your Son Jesus Christ. I confess that He is Lord and I accept Christ as my own personal Savior and according to His Word, right now I am saved. I bind my mind to the mind of Christ and I bind my will to the will of Christ. I declare that I am a child of the Kingdom and will do the will of my Father. Amen.*

I encourage you to let God direct you to a church where you can get discipleship. You are now a part of the Kingdom of marvelous light and the enemy will not give up. You are now a threat to him and he will try to win you back. Surround yourself with people who will encourage you and be supportive in your decision to follow Christ. In you and be supportive in your decision to follow Christ. In your difficult times, don't forget to tag team your DADDY, He will always come in and fight your battles. No matter how tough it gets, NEVER GIVE UP. The race is not for the swift but for those who endure to the end. To my newfound sister in Christ. I see you, baby girl. You are a WINNER!

And then all of a sudden she changed,
That broken little princess was completely rearranged.
This girl was now transformed into a beautiful Queen,
Her mind was renewed and she was able to see.

Radiance escaped whenever she entered a room,
She was royalty, no longer Cinderella;
She wasn't in need of a broom.
The girl once crippled, was now soaring like an eagle,
She was restored, determined, willing and eager.

How lovely, fair and radiant is she,
All the men stared for she possessed something they had never
seen. She is a wonder, a beauty a sight to behold,
No longer garbage, as she had been told.
Stop the search party! The Queen has been found,
She is free at last, and no longer bound.
-Shaniqua L. Howell

The End

To My Boaz

Proverbs 18:22 *He who finds a wife finds a good thing, and obtains favor from the Lord.*

I have written a few letters to my dearest future husband, and have decided to share some of them with you.

Dear Future Husband,

I have kissed a few frogs trying to find you. But when God finally brings us together, I have intentions of slapping you silly for not following the directions and keeping me waiting. (HAHA) When I think about how much of myself I've sacrificed for men who never cared about me to begin with, it solidifies the 10 billion reasons I have decided to wait on you. I patiently and sometimes impatiently wait for the day we meet. No longer will I date copies of you. Wasting your love on those who are not even close enough will never be a problem for me anymore.

I had to give up the life I had planned in order to receive the one God had in store for me; that's you! I can't wait to steal your heart and your last name. I am thankful for my pain, heartache, struggles and the hiccups along the way. Because of it all, it has made me into the wife that you will one day love and cherish. I will, however, never let the past dictate or contaminate our future together. The brokenness has allowed my heart to be healed so the love you will give me will be accepted and not taken for granted.

With my past over I look forward to my future knowing that you will be in it. I don't ask for a fairytale, I am well aware that magic doesn't make a marriage work but hard work does, and I am ready to fight side by side with you as long as you're game. You are a very blessed man. With my presence, it will make you extra blessed. He that findeth a wife (Shaniqua) findeth a good thing. Even the Word says it. I feel honored to know that I will be your helper. I am ready to come and help you work. My bags are packed (just kidding). (HAHA) To my Boaz, until the day you come and redeem me, I await you.

Your Future Wife

Dear Future Husband,

I was the girl who always wanted to bring something to her marriage. I wanted to be able to contribute to our union so the entire burden wouldn't be on you. When I was told that your arrival was at hand, I got sad. I was excited and full of joy at the fact that you were on your way, yet unhappy because I was not going to get the chance to bring anything but myself to the table. I started to contemplate on my life at present. I had no job, no house, no car, no land, and no money in the bank and I was 29 being supported by my dad. I remember crying one particular night and calling up one of my mentors and explaining how I felt. After the conversation I felt a little better but I couldn't shake the fact that I didn't have anything to give to you. It was then God showed up and slapped me upside the head. He took me to my favorite book in the Bible, the book of Ruth.

This woman was a broke foreigner who was in a very bad financial state. She went into the fields to glean what was left over by the reapers. How pathetic was that? She was also a widow who took on the responsibility of a mother-in- law. Boaz saw Ruth's work ethic, a woman of worth, a woman of virtue, a woman of strength and focus, goal- oriented and driven, loyal and committed. Despite her being penniless He saw something in her. He looked pass all the other women in Judah and decided to marry the poor, penniless foreigner.

God spoke to me that night and changed my whole perspective on things. I no longer saw myself as a burden to you but as the woman of virtue who will add to your life and not subtract from it. I rest assured in God that if He has decided to bring us together He will supply all of our needs. Meanwhile, I may have no job as yet to contribute monetarily but I do have work to do- Kingdom work. So although I anxiously await your arrival, for now, I rest peacefully knowing that you are also kingdom working.

Your Future Wife

Dear Future Husband,

After time spent you will come to the understanding that I'm not your average woman. Duh! I'm one of a kind. (lol) Because of the vow I've made unto God, I have plenty of boundaries listed for you to ensure those vows are never broken. Us staying pure before God is very important to me and I'm confident it will be the same for you.

- Absolutely NO SEX before marriage (any form of sex).

- No fondling (I am not a piece of meat).

- I will not be kissing until my wedding day. I know this one may be somewhat of a shocker to you but it's something I desire and it's not up for discussion, however, forehead and on the cheek kisses are allowed. See! There you go, that's my compromise. (HAHA)

- We must always make sure Christ is at the center of our relationship.

- No idolizing of each other at any point.

- Time should always be found for prayer and studying the Word together. Praying together is one of the most intimate things we can do. I know that you will pray with me and not prey on me.

- Accountability figures should be set in place for both of us.

- Holding hands is allowed (I'm not that bad (smile).

- While courting, we will not go to each other's apartment and spend hours on the couch; cuddling leads to fondling, fondling leads to broken vows.

Knowing that I will eventually grow in love with you will make it difficult at times when temptations come our way. I ask that no matter what, we will always put the importance of our purity and vows to God as priority.

Your Future Wife

Dear Future Husband,

I am not the Bonnie to your Clyde; I'm not that type of woman. I am not your ride or die. If you want me to go somewhere with you, then I have some questions. Where are we going? What is your vision? What are your plans for the future? Many people want a love like Bonnie and Clyde or Romeo and Juliet, but as for me, I desire a love like the one Christ has for His church. I don't want someone who will give me a potion and ask me to kill myself. I need someone who will take me to scripture and tell me that we have to die to self daily. I don't want someone who will encourage me to rob a bank with them, but someone who will get on their knees and pray that God supply any need that we may have.

You see, I am definitely not your Bonnie or your Juliet. I am the Woman of Virtue you have asked God to bless you with. I'm the mother of your future children and the helper who will make your life richer. You are my beloved and I am yours. I am also not the Minnie to your Mickey. They have been dating for all these years and still aren't married as yet. Long engagements are for people who don't know what they want. I suggest that you know what you want and get to work. My desire is not a big house, but a home. In our house, we will do Jesus, love, second chances, forgiveness, grace, I'm sorrys and lots of prayer. Our children will never be raised to see the dryness of a house but the love of a home.

We may not have it all together, but together we will have it all. I want you to love God more than you love me. I have no problem taking the backseat. When you place all your love on God I know that you will also lavish me in that same love. I am assured that you will love me great because you love God greater. To my Adam, your rib is calling, can't you hear? My prayer for you is that God may give you a double portion of strength. Your wife is a handful. Just kidding, or maybe not. *SMILE* Man of God, Man of integrity, Man of purpose, Man of vision, I await you.

P.S I prayed away all those girlfriends; you'll thank me later.

Your Future Wife

Dear Future Husband,

One day, despite my flaws and all the other women around, you will look at me and say "She's the one." I thank God for all the jokers that came into my life. I am now able to decipher a clown from a true king. To the husband God has for me, I will wait for you.

Your Future Wife

Examine Thyself

After reading this book, here are some questions I would like you to ask yourself, while being honest and truthful. If the answers are not what they should be, I implore you to take the necessary steps in changing the situation.

1. Have you put your life on hold until marriage?

2. Is your desire for a husband taking precedence over your relationship with Christ?

3. Baggage from past relationships can be extremely detrimental to any future relationship you may have. Are you currently carrying any soul baggage from former relationships?

4. ARE YOU SINGLE?

5. Have you broken your biological clock, or is it still ticking and trying to override the voice of the Holy Spirit?

6. What is more important to you, purpose or marriage?

7. How do you see yourself? Are you made in God's image and His likeness, or do you see yourself as what man says you ought to be?

8. Are you more concerned about having a wedding or a marriage? Most women are caught up with the idea of the wedding not realizing that it's only one day.

9. Where does your focus lie?

10. Have you forgiven the people who have caused you any pain in the past?

11. Have you set your boundaries for when that man comes along?

12. What are you looking for in a man; are you looking for godly character and integrity or will any man do?

13. Ask yourself: "Am I really ready to be in a relationship?"

14. Are you choosing a mate based on your emotions, or is it by the leading of the Holy Spirit?

15. How is your relationship with Christ?

A Virtuous Woman

(Proverbs 31: 10-31)

What is a woman?

Someone we should admire, She should not be treated badly,
Or called out for cheap hire
She is my mother, my sister, your wife
She should not be caught up in the midst of strife

What is a Woman?

A hard worker, a comforter, a friend She will stand by
your side until the very end
Her shoulders are broad, she can take the pain
That doesn't mean you should treat her with disdain.

What is a Woman?

She is happy, industrious and kind,
A woman like this is very hard to find
Whatever she touches is prosperous and good
With or without a husband, she behaves as she should

What is a Woman?

She is gentle, beautiful and wise
All of these characters some will despise
It doesn't matter, because she is made of tough stuff
Don't get me wrong, she knows when she's had enough

What is a Woman?

She is not jealous of what other women achieve For in her heart, she
knows in whom she believes She believes in Jehovah Rapha,
Jehovah Nissi, Jehovah Jireh
She knows that God is good and a great provider

What is a Woman?

She knows when she is hurting and everything seems bad
That she can get on her knees and stand up feeling glad
Her children will one day look up to her and call her blessed
She hardly gets flustered, she hardly gets stressed

What is a Woman?

She carries herself with dignity and grace ,
No one ever has to put her in her place
You will never find her gossiping on the phone
And no demon on earth will enter her home Again;
I ask what is a woman? She is devout and true
What is a woman? She is YOU, YOU, YOU
~Tamara Yearwood~

References

Basic Introduction to Soul Ties
<http://www.greatbiblestudy.com/soulties.php>Copyrighted©
2003-2008 Robert L. and its licensors

Valotton, Kris. Purity, the New Moral Revolution. Pennsylvania:
Destiny Image Publishers Inc. 2008

C. L. Scott . 2014 Sep 24, Dr. Myles Munroe "The Myth of
Singleness Pt.1.Retrieved from
<https://www.youtube.com/watch?v=Br_wKPL3LWs>

Bynum, Juanita. No More Sheets, The Truth About Sex. Lanham
,Maryland: Pneuma Life Publishing . 1998

Hammond, Mckinney Michelle. Sassy Single & Satisfied. Eugene
Oregon: Harvest House Publishers. 2010

Made in the USA
Monee, IL
07 July 2026